Unleashing HER

Redefining Success for Female Entrepreneurs

"Let us not become weary in doing good, for at the proper time we will reap a harvest if we do not give up."

- Galatians 6:9

Dr. Kimberly Olson

Along with 40 Inspiring Female Authors

All Rights Reserved, The Goal Digger Girl

Unleashing HER

Redefining Success for Female Entrepreneurs

Copyright © 2023 by Kimberly Olson

Cover Designed by Abby Ascencio

Photo Credit: Chelsea Patricia

All rights reserved.

www.TheGoalDiggerGirl.com

ISBN- 979-8-9856496-3-5

No part of this publication may be reproduced, stored in a retrieval system or transmitted in any way by any means, electronic, mechanical, photocopy, recording or otherwise without the prior permission of the author except as provided by USA copyright law.

The information provided within this book is for general informational purposes only. While the author worked diligently to keep the information up-to-date and correct, there are no representations or warranties, express or implied, about the completeness, accuracy, reliability, suitability or availability with respect to the information, products, services, or related graphics contained in this book for any purpose. Any use of this information is at your own risk.

The author makes no implications, warranties, promises, suggestions, projections, representations, or guarantees with respect to future prospects or earnings. Any earnings or income statements, or any earnings or income examples, are only estimates of what could be possible to earn. There is no assurance you will do as well as stated in any examples. Any and all claims or representations as to income and earnings are not to be considered as "average earnings".

CONTENTS

Foreword   7

Goal Digger Dedication   12

Introduction   13

Part 1: Transforming Your Mindset

Redefining Who YOU Are – Rebecca Gage   19

Let Go & Let God – Brenda Joy Stabenow   28

An Abundant Mindset – Sydney Crowe   34

Crushing Limiting Beliefs – Karena Moss   42

Part 2: Recalibrating for Success

Successful Embodiment in Manifestation – Kim McGuire   52

Perfectly Imperfect – Dyan Moeller   61

The Power of Wealth Acclimation – Joanna Gard   68

Rewire Your Brain for Success – Dr. Sharon DeHope   76

Part 3: Life Lessons that Last

It's All in God's Timing – Allyson Mancini   84

Creating a Leadership Lifestyle – Trienne Topp — 94

Getting into the Driver's Seat – Jessica Perry — 102

Overcoming Imposter Syndrome – Becky Lafave — 112

Part 4: Casting a New Vision for Your Life

The Power of Daydreaming – Rebecca Pruett — 123

Rooted in Faith – Dr. Amy Nussbaum — 131

Small Steps, Big Wins – Trisha Langford — 137

Leading Yourself First – Mary Kate Berry — 143

Part 5: Setting Your Social Media on Fire

Massive Audience Growth through Consistency – Stephanie Lafler — 154

Authentically Ausome – Alyece Smith — 164

Automation Domination – Raenell Edsall-Taylor — 171

Leading a Winning Team – Wendy Kat — 178

Embrace Your Authentic Power – Sarah Glenn — 186

Sales Success Secrets – Rianna Drummond — 193

Part 6: Conquering Productivity

Set Yourself Up for Success – Courtney Koenig	202
Getting Tech to Work for YOU – Steph Dakin	208
Slow & Steady Wins the Business Growth Game – Pamela Hilton	214
Organizational Tools for Peak Productivity – Abby Ascencio	222
Wearing the Hat YOU Want to Wear – Andrya Martin	231

Part 7: Methods that Monetize

List Leverage Lifestyle – Lindsay Sewell	241
Multiple Streams of Income – Tori Edwards	247
Building Your Business in Your Backyard – Gemma Sharp	253
Flipping the Script – Anja Grissom	264

Part 8: Essential Business Fundamentals

Overcoming Limiting Beliefs to Build A Strong Business – Lauren Buckner	278

Creating a Loyal Community – Amy Oostveen   286

Money Management Tips – Marissa Greco   295

Business Finances & Management – Dr. Argie Nichols   302

Your Relationship with Money – Anna Pexa   312

Part 9: Trusting the Pivot

Embracing the Pivot – Lori Barthlow   322

Pivoting Like a BOSS – Laura Caroffino   329

Later is Greater – Brenna Martin   337

Creating a Life You Love – Jennifer Mirt   341

Through Grief Came the Pivot – Erin Roese   348

The Importance of Lifelong Learning – Leigh Ann Chiari   356

Part 10: Unleashing Your Potential

She Believed She Could – Tracy Lane   364

Setting Your Soul on Fire – Dr. Kimberly Olson   374

About the Author   379

FOREWORD

There was a pivotal point in my life when I decided to finally give myself permission to dream big and have the courage to go after those dreams. The truth is, up until that point I wasn't playing to win, but rather, I was playing to not lose. There was a bubbling well of untapped potential begging to be unleashed. My soul's calling scared me, but it was no longer a whisper that tugged on my heartstrings quietly. It grew louder until I could no longer ignore the game God called me to play.

I knew I had so much more purpose and passion to give to the world, and it was in this divine unfolding of building my dream life that I realized that I wanted to work with other women who were ready to unleash their God-sized dreams. Women that were powerful, creative, and impactful visionaries who were the movement-makers, shapeshifters, and leaders in their respective communities and industries.

Women like Kimberly.

This is how Kimberly and I met, and why she later became a client.

A mutual friend connected us when Kimberly was looking for speakers at her first ever in-person event: Like a Goal Digger Conference at The Gaylord Opry in Nashville, Tennessee. There were a casual 300 people attending and Kimberly had some of the most incredible speakers alongside us in the lineup which included pros like Yahya Bakkar, Jessica Higdon, and Erin King.

This wasn't just a conference. This was a reflection of how Kimberly shows up to her dreams.

Over the course of our now coach-client relationship, I've watched her do this over and over again. Her ability to take ideas from inception to production and manifestation is undoubtedly remarkable and, I believe, largely in part to her adept ability to integrate and take action quickly.

From the start it was evident to me that Kimberly is one of the most powerful visionaries I've coached. She is the living embodiment of the saying "from tiny seeds, grow mighty trees" with a deep and profound understanding that her ideas are a reality that has yet to be birthed. Unshakeable in her ability to be decisive and hold to her vision, she knows that dream realized is never a matter of "if," but simply a matter of "when."

Her business inspires other women to do the same, rallied around her by the thousands, where they come into her world through certifications, courses, retreats, workshops, conferences, and now her new book *Unleashing HER: Redefining Success for Female Entrepreneurs*.

This book is also proof of yet another dream manifested, as it is her seventh book in just under seven years.

Inside these pages, you will undoubtedly find yourself among the inspiring stories so that, you too, can lean in to the growth edge and unleash the fullest expression of the woman within to seek out the success you not only know is possible, but inevitable.

Kimberly will not only inspire you, but invite you into seeking out your biggest dreams so you can stop waiting for "one day" and know that today is the best place to start taking action.

I've seen too many women talk themselves out of the very thing they want because of the fear it requires them to overcome. As writer and feminist organizer Gloria Steinem says, *"dreaming, after all, is a form of planning."*

What if, in fact, our dreams were already a reality we simply have to start taking action toward?

One thing I've noticed about every successful woman I've encountered is their willingness to live on the edge between their current reality and their next biggest dream. They know that it is only the limitations of their mind that hold them back, and so the deeper initiation exists in challenging the limitations.

They work with dedication and commitment toward cultivating an unf*ckwithable self-trust, defining an intrinsic sense of self-worth, and stepping into a sisterhood of women who normalize their bold and "unrealistic" dreams. With pillars of support like this, they are able to go beyond their edges becoming the successful woman they know they are capable of being – *the woman unleashed.*

Keri Ford

Founder & CEO of *Elevate with Keri*, Podcast Show Host of *Literally First Class*

www.ElevateWithKeri.com

GOAL DIGGER DEDICATION

To all of my Goal Diggers who want to learn how to tap into their limitless potential. You aspire to create more in your life and aren't afraid to dream. You know you have it in you to change your family tree, and I am positive you will see yourself in these women's stories. Let them be the inspiration you need to unapologetically go after your dreams!

xo,

Kimberly

INTRODUCTION

And he said to them, *"Follow me, and I will make you fishers of men."* -**Matthew 4:19**

I love this verse so much because it aligns so deeply with my calling in this world. I didn't always know I'd dedicate my life to teaching and inspiring others to create the life they've always dreamed of, but if I look back I can see clues throughout my life.

When I was in elementary school, I remember gathering the neighborhood kids around our old, weathered picnic table and handing out bright plastic yellow folders. You know the ones I'm talking about. We were all assigned jobs and worked together to come up with fun games and even built a fort outside.

Into adulthood I always found myself in leadership roles, even becoming a director of a multimillion dollar company when I was only 26. I just love bringing people together and showing them the roadmap so they can learn, stretch and grow.

And that brings me to the present day. Although I had dedicated the past two decades to speaking across North

America, appearing on television over a hundred times, sharing what I'd learned while getting two PhDs in Natural Health and Holistic Nutrition, something shifted.

As I was clawing my way out of six figures of debt and learning online marketing so I could quit my job and be home for my babies, I realized I was really good at business. Not just teaching social media…but all of it. Anything to do with making money.

Soon, others were asking me to coach them, and in 2018, *Goal Digger Girl Co* was born. We've grown that company to a global coaching program serving thousands of female entrepreneurs all around the world building their own businesses online.

I've made a LOT of mistakes running a multimillion dollar company. I've cried more times than I'd like to admit. I've hired several coaches of my own because I was ready to burn it all down. And in that process, I've learned so much. I feel myself quantum leaping over and over again.

There are so many things I wish I had known going into this. I really wish I could have sat beside the women in this book and shared stories with them. Lessons we could pass along and glean insight from one another. And most importantly, to realize we are not alone.

Being an entrepreneur can be very lonely. There is a lot of self-doubt, imposter syndrome and self-sabotage that can creep in while we're innocently scrolling social media. If we're not careful, we can talk ourselves right out of this vision we have for ourselves and our families.

That is why I wanted to put this collaboration together. I wanted you to have a place to go to if you need a bit of encouragement or just want to know that you're not alone.

You can read this book in order, or browse the topics outlined at the beginning and go to whatever area you're called to right now. I will kick off each section with my two cents and then you'll see several chapters from our amazing contributing authors after that.

In addition, we've put together an entire book resources section online full of additional content from our contributing authors that will allow you to go even deeper with the content they've shared. You can find it at **https://TheGoalDiggerGirl.com/Unleashing-Her-Book/**

My hope is that your life is changed in some way. It can be big or small, but I want to leave you better off than when you first picked up this book. If you do have any powerful breakthroughs or insights, feel free to send me a DM. I'd love to hear your favorite takeaways!

Part 1: Transforming Your Mindset

One day I'll write a single book all about mindset, but for now, I'd just like to remind you that it's always mindset before mechanics.

Whether you aren't making sales within your business, or you're not getting the audience growth you'd like, it's your mindset. This can be hard to admit because we trick ourselves by saying, *"But Kimberly, I'm doing allllll the things. Where's my money??"*

I totally get it. I really do. And I am going to gently nudge you to realize that it comes down to your belief of those things happening for you. You have to get clear on what you want, envision it, stay aligned vibrationally and expect it to come into the physical reality.

That's it. So dive into this chapter to learn from those that have transformed their own mindsets.

CHAPTER 1

Redefining Who YOU Are

by Rebecca Gage

Deep inside the heart of every woman is a beautiful, intricate tale of the past woven into the present - a history that shapes who she is that deserves to be etched in time.

A Story of HER.

Each story is different, and yet, they all have something in common. Two veins running simultaneously, parallel to one another, each occurring at the exact same moment.

A legend of old…

Good vs Evil

Light vs Dark

Truth vs Lie

Life vs Death

The way you choose to see your story is up to you. You can choose a version that is empowered, one where you see God and the Universe in every aspect. Or you can choose a disempowered version of victimhood and defeat. My invitation to you is that, through my story, you allow a new version to emerge. A new vein to come to the surface. I invite you to go beyond the veneer and peel the layers back one by one.

It's time to see what else is there. It's time to activate the greatest and purest version of you. I invite you to see God in your story. A crack of light, a glimpse of Heaven. In every detail of your story.

HE IS THERE.

Pain. Trauma. Neglect.

My life growing up felt out of control. I lived in dysfunction. Both of my parents were alcoholics. As the eldest of three girls, much of my childhood was spent looking after my two younger sisters. My earliest memories include missing birthday parties, not being able to play with my friends, and being forced to grow up too soon.

Alcohol. Fear. Chaos.

My head was on a swivel. I learned how to decipher in a few words between minor arguments and all-out brawls between my parents. I deduced from the way they walked through the door of our double-wide trailer whether they were completely intoxicated, or merely buzzed. I understood very early on when I needed to step in for my mom or prevent my sisters from getting caught in the crossfire. I gauged when I could let them be. But *I* was never able to be; I was always on high alert.

Because of the constant bickering, fighting, strife, and CHAOS, it all felt SO LOUD! I had to become very quiet. Not seen, not heard. I learned that I had to water down who I was to keep the turbulence at bay. I always felt that I was TOO MUCH and this too-muchness might push my parents too far. Moreover, it was from this lens that I began to see the world around me.

Unworthy. Unwanted. Unloveable.

I tried to fix the constant fighting, drinking, and chaos the only way I knew how - I desperately wanted to right the wrongs that weren't mine. Do good in school, work hard, get good grades. (But don't shine too much.) A balancing act that cost so much, but worth keeping my family together. Perhaps my parents would see me. Perhaps they would love me.

As a freshman in high school, I received my first "C" on my report card. Unbeknownst to me, the negative impact of this night would prove to be one that is forever engraved on my heart. I came home around dinner time that night. As I turned down the street, I could hear loud music coming from our trailer; we had family visiting that weekend. It was a special time as they came from two hours away to enjoy a weekend in the mountains - riding horses, fishing, and a much needed break from the city.

I knew my dad seeing my report card could go one of two ways. I figured he would be upset, but with family there, possibly it could go unnoticed. However, as I cautiously made my way up the stairs of the front porch I knew immediately from the look in his eyes, that one, he was drunk, and two, this was going to be bad. When my dad saw my report card, he flew into a rage. He told me I was a loser, a low-life, and that I was going nowhere. Because of this, a huge argument ensued between my dad and all the visiting family.

After our visitors left to drive home late that night, my intoxicated parents and I sat down as a family. I told my mom that if she didn't quit drinking I would never speak to her again. I meant it. I couldn't handle it anymore. Mom turned to my dad and said, *"We need to quit drinking, for our family."*

Dad replied, *"Well if you are giving me the choice between my family and alcohol, I choose alcohol."* I. CHOOSE. ALCOHOL. Those three words reverberated in my mind. My heart shattered that night and I would cling to those three words for many decades as evidence... as truth...as my life story.

"I choose alcohol," interpreted as *"I DON'T CHOOSE YOU,"* meant that I was unworthy; I was unwanted; I was unlovable. Or so I thought.

Divorce. Abuse. Addiction

That night, I stopped and started many things. I stopped trying to keep my family together. I stopped trying to intervene between my parents. I stopped trying to hold it all together. I stopped this balancing act. Two years of bitter ugliness - restraining orders, Dad threatening to kill Mom, and finally the divorce was final.

I started down a very dark, downward spiral that wouldn't end for years. I started coping and numbing the only way I knew how. I began with alcohol, but soon was experimenting with much harder, and much worse, drugs. Looking back now, I realize the escalation was rapid because my longing was to feel no pain. I started to like feeling numb. And with that came an accelerated progression through many substances, each worse than the last.

I was haunted by the words my dad spoke to me that night. The deeper I could lower myself into the pit, the further I was from the impact of those three blows. My nightmare was the disempowered version of my story allowing me to believe I was a victim and defeated.

Perhaps some of you have a difficult story, too. Maybe you're still seeing through the lens of anger, bitterness, fear, and rejection. However, I invite you to zoom out. Look in the peripheral for the other emerging vein. What else was there? Can you see it?

I asked God to show me where **HE** was and why **HE** had abandoned me that night. And something incredible began to happen…I began to see it. A crack of Light. A glimpse of Heaven. I began to see **HIM** all throughout my life.

My focus had been entirely on the words and actions of my father and I didn't realize there was another story that was being created at that exact moment. It's always been there. One that was pure - full of struggle, triumph, and great love.

Triumph. Unconditional Love. Enlightenment.

It was the parallel vein. A narrative unlike that of the first. And it happened at the exact same moment. Blinded by the deep wounds inflicted upon me, I could not see God. But as I zoomed out, I saw another story… another vein emerged. I saw a mom who chose her daughters without question. I saw a mom who walked away from shackles of her own to break cycles; even though she was scared and didn't know how she would do it, even though this was the only life she had ever known… I saw that she chose ME.

And if I zoomed out even a little more, I would also see another crack of Light…I would see a man, yet a boy, who had become a father. A little boy who had experienced pain, trauma, and abuse of his own, doing the best he could with what he knew.

My enlightenment came because I chose to let go and invite God into those dark and difficult parts of my story. I chose a new lens - one of forgiveness and love. I understand how my past has shaped the woman I am, but it doesn't have the power to define me. Only I have the power to do that.

When trauma happens, it creates different versions of us. Versions that may not be the truest interpretation. But that doesn't mean you have to stay there; a much better story exists. Ask God to show you the truth.

Allow…

HIS vein to emerge.

HIS truth to empower you.

HIS love to guide you.

Will you accept this invitation? Will you allow a crack of light in? Will you allow a glimpse of heaven to come through in every single iteration of your story? You get to decide.

Rebecca Gage, a Transformation Coach and Success Mentor, is a coach to successful entrepreneurs and business women who are ready to step into their full power and unlock their greatest potential.

She is the CEO and founder of her company, *Rebecca Gage Coaching,* and the host of her show, *Elevate.* She's a passionate speaker, teacher, and trainer who pours into every woman she meets. Rebecca owes all of her success in business, finance, and life, to God, her disciplined studies of personal development, and practice of self-love.

Rebecca is a wife and a mom to four children; two girls and two boys. She and her family reside in the beautiful Rocky Mountains of Colorado, and you will often find her outside enjoying the majestic scenery, playing, and creating in whatever facet she can.

CHAPTER 2

Let Go & Let God

by Brenda Joy Stabenow

How boring is your life? Do you feel like you've barely recovered since being hit with all the trauma from 2020? You're tired, overwhelmed, and your world is spinning fast. Maybe you feel like you are stuck in the same place you were a year ago: your life just isn't that exciting.

I'm going to be very bold and blunt with you, because I've been there. Life is too short, too precious, and God has called you to something bigger. Do not let Him down. It's time to revive the joy in your life and your business. Are you ready for a revival? I'm going to give you tips and strategies that helped me surrender to God and grow a thriving business.

"I lie in the dust; revive me by your word." Psalm 119:25.

God has a plan for you to prosper, to give you hope and a future (Jeremiah 29:11). Don't quit! I understand your discouragement. When I had my chocolate business, we had a storefront as well as an online business. At least once a year I'd think about giving up and closing it all due to feeling completely wiped out, stressed, and missing my family.

One year I decided to get intentional with increasing online sales. The most important decision I made was to give it all to God and make Him the CEO of my life and business. I learned to surrender to Him daily. "*After you have suffered a little while, He'll restore, support, and strengthen you, and He will place you on a firm foundation.*" 1 Peter 5:10. He led me to new revelations. His way is better!

I had lost joy in my life and needed a revival. I should have hired more help sooner than I did, and the business would have grown a lot faster. Revival means to live again, awaken, improve. Stay in your zone of genius and God will multiply it. Hire out the rest. God doesn't call the qualified, He qualifies the called. Are you ready to accept His call?

God started showing me new ways that I could learn and grow. I took a variety of courses, attended conferences, hired a coach, and through the power of social media, increased our online sales by 2800%. I was 52 years old when I started learning all of this; age is just a number!

One of the greatest examples of this truth about age can be found in the story of the life of Abraham. At the age of 75, God called Abraham to leave his country, his people, and found a new nation. Abraham obeyed God's call and journeyed to the land of Canaan. Despite his old age and lack of children, God promised Abraham that He would become the father of many nations, his "seed" would inherit the land and that God would bless him and his descendants. Even though he faced many obstacles, Abraham continued to trust God's plan for his life. Eventually God fulfilled his promise and Abraham became the father of Isaac, who was the father of Jacob, and the twelve tribes of Israel. Where have you been putting your trust?

Flash forward three years, I sold my business to a family that I had prayed about and who loved the business as much as I did. My manager, Liz, whom I loved and adored, had worked for me since she was 15 years old. One of the proudest moments I have is training and encouraging her to rise up into business ownership. After she purchased the company, I was then able to move my whole family South to live the life we always wanted.

"Those who trust in the Lord will find new strength and soar high on wings like eagles. They will run and not grow weary." Isaiah 40:31.

I owned my chocolate business for 21 years, which doesn't seem possible. Most businesses don't make it past the five-year mark. Data from the US Bureau of Labor Statistics shows that approximately 20% of new businesses fail during the first two years, 45% during the first five years, and 65% during the first ten years. Only 25% of new businesses make it to 15 years! Business ownership is hard, especially when you do it without God.

It took years of doing hard things that I never imagined having to do. Stamina, grit, perseverance, a big love and passion for the business, plus a supportive husband, helped. Recently I heard, *"Don't do work for God, without doing the work WITH God."* If only I'd known this sooner.

Cash flow is crucial for every business, and I was determined to make my business thrive and survive. This meant that, in the beginning, we were open on holidays. One Easter, I had just finished up with the little kids as they collected their Easter eggs from around our home. I was in a hurry to open my store before the rush of customers came in. As I was leaving our neighborhood I watched, with tears streaming down my face, families all dressed up, laughing, smiling, and taking pictures on their front porch. I was doing "hard things" so my business would make it. Remember, like Dave Ramsey says, *"If you will live like no one else, later you can live like no one else."*

Surrendering to God is powerful. Here's a few tips that can help you, G.O.D:

G - Give it to God. Every morning sit in silence with your Bible, pray to Him and ask Him to guide your steps. Write out the scripture you feel drawn to.

O - Obey God. When you surrender to Him, read His word, pray and worship, you'll gain a deep relationship with Him and start hearing Him speak. OBEY his commands. Love Him and love thy neighbor. (Matthew 22:36-39)

D - Do the work. He can give you all the wisdom you need, but if you don't take any action nothing will change. Do what moves the needle forward. *"Pray like it depends on God but work like it depends on you."* – Dave Ramsey

God's promise for your life is not limited by age or past failures. Trust God's plan even if it seems impossible. His Word is the best operations manual, so use it. Bring heaven on earth. *"Do not trust human wisdom but in the power of God."* 1 Corinthians 2:5. When you say, *"I don't know what to do,"* you aren't stepping into leadership. You're really saying, *"I'm not willing to make a decision."* Get that stinkin' thinkin' out of your head; you can't create new beginnings with old beliefs. God wants you to grow and develop the gifts He gave you and for you to keep learning and evolving. His plan is not static. You are one of a kind - no one else out there has your unique DNA. Do not waste it! You are worthy and redeemed. Keep moving forward, it's not too late.

Brenda is a 23-year veteran entrepreneur. She built a thriving brick and mortar chocolate business for 21 years that she expanded and grew online all while raising her four spicy kids. Her dream came true when she sold her successful company in 2021 and moved her family from the great Midwest to Florida. Now she helps other female entrepreneurs build their businesses so they can live a life they love. Her CEO is God.

CHAPTER 3

An Abundant Mindset

by Sydney Crowe

An abundance mindset...that is not something that has come easily to me. It's something that I have had to learn, cultivate and maintain over the years. If I am being honest with you, it has only been in the last 3 years that I have learned the true meaning of it, how to create it, and how to honor it.

For the majority of my adult life, I really didn't know my own inner compass. I remember being told I had to go to college and at 17- & 18-years-old not even knowing what classes to take. So, naturally, I took what my best friend at the time was taking. That didn't pan out for a number of reasons. I ended up getting four different diplomas over the years and currently do not use any of them in my career. That's not to say they weren't good learning blocks, it's just to say that I have naturally struggled with my own direction.

The one thing I was certain of was marrying my husband, but again that didn't stop me from trying to self-sabotage that in the beginning. I knew then what I have proven today, and that was that we could build a beautiful life together with children and the whole nine yards.

We were blessed with our first daughter in 2013. In the beginning, we had a lot of health scares with her and that was the start of my anxiety. After the first few months things seemed to level off, but when our second daughter arrived in 2015 my anxiety took a turn for the worse, and our oldest started to struggle with some behavioral issues.

Over the following five years, I struggled mentally to manage it all. From the outside looking in we had a picture-perfect life, and have been very fortunate. So why did I keep waking up wondering if this was all life had to offer? Why was it not enough for me? I felt so much guilt and shame around that, that I wasn't even being honest with anyone around me. I was scared that they would judge me as an unfit mother. It was another moment in my life where I was unsure of the path to take and what to do. Why wasn't it enough? Well I can tell you now that it's because I was letting life happen *to* me instead of believing that it was happening *for* me.

So what changed...? I was introduced to the world of personal development and coaching. At the end of 2020, I listened in on a Zoom call and the energy for me was palpable. It really was this feeling of being brought back to life. I knew instantly that it was a missing piece that I needed in my life, and I have surrounded myself with communities of powerful women ever since.

The reason I tell you this piece of my backstory is because it highlights the fact that I lived with a scarcity mindset for the majority of my life. That doesn't mean that my life was scarce, but my mindset was. It shows that if I can change a lifetime of conditioning, a lifetime of a single identity that I lived with, and create an abundance mindset, then anyone can.

So what is an abundance mindset? Well by definition it is the belief that there is plenty out there for everyone in the world. How does one cultivate an abundance mindset? The first step is recognizing the limiting beliefs and mindset patterns you have. It requires a deep level of self-awareness and introspection. Limiting beliefs are the deeply ingrained thoughts and perceptions we hold about ourselves and the world that hinder our progress and potential. They often stem from past experiences, societal conditioning, or negative self-talk. By paying attention to our thoughts, emotions, and recurring patterns of behavior, we can begin to identify these limiting beliefs. It involves questioning the validity and accuracy of our beliefs and challenging the negative narratives that hold us back. By recognizing and acknowledging these self-imposed limitations, we open ourselves up to new possibilities and opportunities for growth. Through self-reflection, mindfulness, and a willingness to embrace change, we can gradually replace these limiting beliefs with empowering ones, cultivating a positive and growth-oriented mindset.

Gratitude plays a crucial role in developing an abundance mindset, as it shifts our focus from scarcity to abundance and opens us up to the possibilities that surround us. When we practice gratitude, we acknowledge and appreciate the blessings, big or small, in our lives. This practice helps us recognize the abundance that already exists, leading to a sense of fulfillment and contentment. Cultivating gratitude can be achieved through various techniques such as keeping a gratitude journal, where we write down things we are thankful for each day, or expressing gratitude directly to others. Additionally, taking time to reflect on the positive aspects of challenging situations can help us shift our focus and perspective. By reframing our thoughts and looking for the lessons, or silver linings, we empower ourselves to see opportunities where we once saw obstacles. Ultimately, gratitude has the power to transform our mindset, enabling us to embrace abundance and attract more positive experiences into our lives.

Maintaining and sustaining an abundance mindset is crucial for personal growth and success. Overcoming obstacles and setbacks is an integral part of this mindset, as it allows you to view challenges as opportunities for growth and learning. Surrounding yourself with positive influences, such as supportive friends and mentors, can greatly impact your mindset and outlook on life. Additionally, adopting daily practices for nurturing and strengthening an abundance mindset is essential. These practices may include gratitude exercises, visualization, affirmations, and seeking out inspiring and motivational content. By consistently embracing these strategies, individuals can cultivate and maintain an abundance mindset, leading to greater fulfillment and achievement in all areas of life.

I want to highlight the importance of that last paragraph because mindset work is never finished. It is always something that we need to be conscious of and maintain. There will be moments or events that can rock you, some right to your core, and that is when it is most important to be consistent with your daily practices.

I'll share my story with you of how I almost lost all my hard work over the last few years. It was January of 2022 and I received a call from one of my daughter's doctors. We finally had received a concrete diagnosis of Wiedemann-Steiner Syndrome. While I was somewhat relieved to have an answer, the fact that this was life-long and could be passed to her children one day, plus all of the other things that could go along with it was one of those moments that rocked me to my core. *All of a sudden I felt life happening TO me again instead of FOR me.* I forgot and neglected the tools that I had so diligently cultivated.

My limiting beliefs took control and I felt lost for a short while. I am grateful that I was surrounded by my loving husband with whom I was able to lean on, and the incredible communities of badass women in my life who inspire me and allow me to be raw with them. I have to give credit where credit is due. I am so grateful and inspired by my little girl, who has taken this diagnosis and is determined to not let anything hold her back from her goals. By seeing her determination, I was able to get back to my daily practices and became a Mindset Coach so that I could help others. Sometimes we need to borrow others' beliefs until we can believe it ourselves, and that is why a strong community is so crucial in those moments of doubt.

An abundance mindset is something that you need to work on. If you neglect it, it will neglect you. Always practice gratitude, even if at that moment it is just for another day of living. Who and what you surround yourself with matters immensely. Staying connected to a positive community that you can lean on and that will remind you of your tools when you are feeling low will help beyond measure. Lastly, take time for yourself to really know who you are and where you are going. Journaling, meditations, and all of the other tools will allow you to give yourself clarity and grace.

Sydney Crowe is a mindset mastery coach and mental wellness advisor. As a mom and successful entrepreneur, she understands the unique challenges faced by women trying to balance motherhood and business ownership. Raising a neuro-divergent daughter has allowed her a unique set of skills in that area. Sydney provides practical strategies and mindset shifts to help her clients increase their confidence, productivity, and profits and empowers mompreneurs to turn their passion into profit and create a life they love for themselves and their families. She lives with her husband of 13 years (18, really) and two daughters in Canmore, AB. They love living in the mountains and enjoying all they have to offer and are very passionate about travel. In the last year Sydney and her family have traveled to four countries, 18 cities/towns showing their kids the world and working from anywhere as they go.

CHAPTER 4

Crushing Limiting Beliefs

by Karena Moss

When God called me to homeschool, I asked him to repeat himself because I thought he had accidentally hit the wrong mic button. Turns out God doesn't call the qualified; He qualifies the called. My mountain of doubt was high, but my vision was crystal clear. I didn't question my purpose; I doubted my ability to accomplish my calling.

So how did I overcome all the limiting beliefs of failure and inadequacy? I put my blinders on, focused on what was in front of me, and turned off the noise surrounding me. I knew God wouldn't abandon me. I discovered that mindset is not a destination, but a daily choice to believe that the success at the end of the story will prove the world wrong.

I could have been paralyzed into inaction because I simply had no idea how to homeschool. I could have listened to the world's doubt, anger, and indignation. But what if the world was wrong and the power of one decision, one mom, one family, could change the trajectory of education? What if I was the last piece in a lock sequence, and my key tumbled all the pieces into place to open the door for others? What would happen if I didn't show up because I was afraid? Was there someone waiting on me to step into my greatness, so they could have the courage to step into theirs?

Purpose always reveals itself through action not stagnation. My conviction to homeschool surpassed my confidence in my ability. If I truly believed the end of the story, then my belief would outweigh any obstacle my mind and the world could create. You have to leap even though you might fail because that's how you find the success waiting on the other side.

Being overwhelmed by all the unknowns is a choice. You need to have faith over fear and conviction over confidence. Limiting yourself only blocks the power within you. Perfection isn't possible, so just start. Quit standing on the high dive platform looking down at the expanse of the deep end repeating to yourself that you can't do it. Jump! I guarantee that once you are swimming, and you've discovered that you are still alive and haven't drowned, your fear will shrink and your confidence will soar.

Being in charge of your own future is freeing! People won't agree with you. Friends will abandon you and family will say mean things. But you have the power to tune out the negative trash talk. I'm sure you've heard the story of Hernàn Cortés. When he landed in what is now Mexico he burned his ships to ensure that his crew had no choice but to follow him inland to conquer the Aztec Empire. He destroyed the safety net. Success or failure– those were the only options.

You have the power to ensure the success or failure of your dreams. Will you let fear stop you? It's time to burn the ships. Learning isn't supposed to be easy. Just like everything in life there are hills and valleys, but it's the process that refines us. Learning isn't a stored box of accomplishments collecting dust while preserving the memories of once great ideas and achievements. Learning should go the distance. As you travel through life you should want to know more, be more, achieve more, impact more.

I don't remember ever thinking that school was fun, except for maybe a hot minute in third grade. Going to school and seeing my friends was great, but the act of learning never seemed exciting. Rather, it was something I *had* to do. And just when I thought I was good at something, there was a teacher to remind me that I wasn't.

Once I started homeschooling, I learned that learning can and should be fun. Ironically, my kids taught me the joy and importance of lifelong learning. I don't have a lot of school memories before third grade, but I do remember that I loved math - until I didn't. Maybe not everyone remembers third grade, but I do. We lived in Virginia at the time and my teacher's name was Mr. Very, who thought I was good at math. Because he believed in me and taught me to carefully write my numbers and solve the problems one step at a time, I believed in myself. I believed that I could learn hard things, do hard things. When third grade ended, we moved to another state, and my self-confidence moved with me.

My fourth grade teacher was old and would march around the room knocking her cane on the floor, but math still made sense and the year ended in success. Then in fifth grade, a wooden board containing rows of nails appeared along with a bag of rubber bands. I think this was an early introduction to geometry. Somehow I was supposed to practice making shapes with my rubber bands, but the point was lost on me. However, I still thought I was smart at the end of fifth grade, although I questioned the value of my shape-making skills.

And then the ground shifted. Sixth grade math happened. One single moment in history changed my belief in learning forever. I asked one question about a story problem that I didn't understand and I was informed in front of the whole class that I was stupid. I was clearly confused, since Mr. Very had thought I was smart and gifted in math, and I was left with no power to argue my case. She was the teacher; she was in charge. Humiliated, I never asked another question. An expert had declared that I was bad at math.

As the years went on I did okay in math, even getting through pre-calculus. I went on to take a three-hour experimental math class in college; disaster is the only word to describe that experience. But I prevailed and was over the moon when I didn't have to take any more math classes. Ironically, I worked in accounts payable at a country club in college, served as a tax consultant at Jackson Hewitt Tax Service, built a network marketing business on the side, and created financial affidavits and reports as a paralegal. Somewhere I must have thought I was still good at math.

And then I started homeschooling. Nothing on the planet can dig up every insecurity you have ever had than when you start homeschooling. Your memories remind you of your shortcomings, and the world reminds you of your failures. Looking back I had put learning aside, thinking I was done with that chapter of my life. I was always an avid reader, but not an intentional learner.

I figured I would learn with my kids as they progressed through school but I had no plans of actively learning – just keeping up with being a mom kept me busy enough! Turns out God has an amazing sense of humor. I started homeschooling my oldest son in 3rd grade. Remember, I thought I was pretty good at math in 3rd grade until I had to explain what the borrowed numbers in subtraction actually meant. Not remembering if I ever learned phonics, I learned it in order to teach my daughter how to read. Suddenly every day was filled with information I had never learned, or forgot that I learned, and it was exciting!

I learned from my son that I could solve a math problem in different ways because there wasn't one way to get the right answer. Not knowing something wasn't a problem; it was the beginning of finding a solution. Road trips, vacations, even fun day trips to the zoo became learning opportunities. I literally went back to school with my kids and it's been amazing. I know that homeschooling created in me a desire that had died in 6th grade - a desire to learn more, do more, be more, impact more. Becoming a lifelong learner is the best addiction there is.

God gave us this magnificent world and brilliant minds to learn, grow and create. I knew my kids were watching me. If I gave up learning, then how could I expect them to study and learn? I read all the books they read, I graded every test, I read every paper. I've studied High School U.S. History more times than I can count. Homeschooling saved me. I thought God had hit the wrong mic button when he called me to homeschool. Turns out He was giving me a do-over. He believed in me, and He thought I was smart. Little did I know that homeschooling would become the most consequential event of my life. Maybe my 6th grade teacher did me a favor that day, because that was when I became a lifelong learner even though I didn't know it at the time. I didn't need someone to teach me; I could learn things on my own. Mr. Very had taught me that I could do hard things.

Karena Moss is a homeschool mom of four kids with over a decade of experience, author of *Leap of Faith* and creator of *Homeschooling Your Way*. After battling constant illness, her oldest son missed about 2/3 of kindergarten, and her youngest daughter had lung surgery due to pneumonia, she was frustrated and discouraged. Then God hit the mic button one morning and told her that homeschooling was the answer. Little did she know that homeschooling would become the most consequential event of her life. She is passionate about health and wellness and helping SAH mompreneurs grow their businesses.

Part 2:

Recalibrating for Success

Continuing on from the foundational concepts of mindset work, we step into the awareness that we need to recalibrate for success.

What does that mean? Well, if you think about it, almost all of our thoughts are the same as the day before and for the most part our subconscious mind is running the show. Therefore, we need to consciously get aligned with success.

Everyone's definition of success is different, as you can see from these chapters. But what does success look like to you? Why is that important to you? What feelings do you want to feel when you are "successful?"

Earl Nightingale famously said, *"We become what we think about most of the time, and that's the strangest secret."* I love this because if that's the case, which I believe it is, then WE are in control of our current reality.

And if it's not what you want it to be, YOU can change it.

CHAPTER 5

Successful Embodiment in Manifestation

by Kim McGuire

Manifestation has become an increasingly popular topic among online entrepreneurs and in the mindset space. If the word manifestation isn't familiar to you, perhaps you have heard it referred to as the Law of Attraction. This is explained as the importance of visualizing your goals, or the concept that we attract what we are an energetic alignment with. While the manifestation process can take on many forms, there is one crucial aspect that is not often talked about - embodiment. Embodying your desires is the missing piece that will be the game changer for your manifestation success. In this chapter, we will explore what embodiment is, the blocks that hinder it, and practical tools to cultivate it in your entrepreneurial journey.

Let me ask you a couple of questions and see if you have thought about what I have in the past about manifestation. Have you ever wondered why when you are manifesting something that you want so deeply, or you perceive as so "big," that it seems like it takes forever to show up in your physical reality? Or why when there is something that you do not want to experience, or that seems silly or simple to you, that it seems to manifest quickly, if not instantly? Think back to a time when you were talking about something you did not want to create…were you filled with emotion and feelings about it? Did it feel like it was in every bit of you and you could feel it in your bones? Did it feel real, even though it was just a thought or concept? Was there any doubt about what you were saying or feeling?

Now think about that "big" thing that you want to manifest or create. Do you feel it and know in your bones that it will happen? Are you filled with certainty in every level of your being? Or is there some doubt because it feels like it's a great idea, but it's not real? I was able to create the junk that I didn't want or care about so easily because, as I now know, I embodied it through and through.

Embodiment is the process of fully integrating your desires into your being, and aligning your thoughts, emotions, beliefs, and actions to create a powerful energetic resonance with your goals and desires. To feel it and know it in your bones, as I like to say. Embodiment is the bridge between your dreams and their physical manifestation. It is about bringing your desires into your body and living them in the present moment. It involves engaging all your senses, emotions, and intuition to create a deep sense of knowing and connection with your goals. When you embody your desires, you become a vibrational match for them, attracting the opportunities and resources needed to make them a reality.

As individuals we all have our unique reasons as to why we may not embody our manifestations and as entrepreneurs (and humans), there are some common blocks that hinder embodiment. Let's take a look at the most common and how to overcome them.

Disconnection: In our fast-paced modern world, and in the realm of online entrepreneurship, you may find yourself disconnected from your body. You'll notice that you're not being present, being connected to your desires, and grounded in who you desire to be. We often live in our heads, consumed by thoughts, and neglecting the wisdom and intelligence of our physical selves. When you operate solely from the digital space, you may find it challenging to embody your intentions and align them with your physical experiences. It may begin to feel outside of you. The rapidly evolving digital landscape and the abundance of tools and platforms can overwhelm online entrepreneurs. This overwhelm can lead to scattered energy, lack of focus, and an inability to align actions with intentions, thereby impeding successful manifestation.

To overcome disconnection, you can create practices that support a realignment of body, mind and spirit throughout your day. Deep breathing exercises, taking frequent breaks to get sunshine and fresh air, and being present to your posture are all ways to be aware of your body during the day. Being aware of how you are feeling as you work and are present online is very supportive to embodiment. Are you feeling resistant to what you are creating? Are you excited and motivated? If you are not aligned emotionally, give yourself permission to take a step back and ask yourself what is creating this block for you? Create the shift and connection you desire.

Limiting Beliefs: Your belief systems shape your reality. Limiting beliefs are ingrained thoughts and perceptions that hold you back from fully embracing your dreams. If you hold limiting beliefs about yourself or the world, they act as blocks to embodiment. Negative self-perception, societal conditioning, fears and past traumas can all contribute to limiting beliefs that impede your ability to fully embody your desires. Unresolved emotional wounds and traumas can also create limiting beliefs and energetic blockages within your body, preventing the smooth flow of energy necessary for manifestation. These blockages often manifest as physical tension, chronic pain, or emotional numbness. Online entrepreneurs may encounter limiting beliefs specific to the digital world, such as imposter syndrome, fear of visibility, or a scarcity mindset regarding competition. These beliefs act as blocks to embodiment, hindering the alignment of our desires with our physical experience and preventing the integration of empowering thoughts, emotions, and actions required for success.

There are many ways to overcome our limiting beliefs. The first step is to acknowledge the belief that is no longer serving you. The next step is declaring that this belief or pattern is no longer serving you or the future version of you that you are manifesting. Then you create a new belief that does serve you. Many beliefs were learned as children and during different phases of life. Our belief systems are like apps and programs on our phones. They run in the background of our thoughts and influence how and why we experience life as we do. In the same way that we upgrade our apps and phone system when there are updates available, we get to update and upgrade our beliefs as we evolve and grow. This is where affirmations, release techniques, forgiveness and the practice of "living as if" can help you create and reprogram a new belief system. Sometimes we can do that on our own and other times we may reach out to a coach or mentor for assistance.

Overemphasis on Strategy: While strategies are crucial for online business success, an overemphasis on strategy alone can lead to a lack of embodiment. When entrepreneurs solely rely on external tactics without fully aligning them with their internal intentions and beliefs, they may experience a disconnect between their efforts and desired outcomes. Merge external strategies with your internal intentions and intuitive guidance. Before implementing any tactic or strategy, take a moment to connect with your desired outcomes and assess whether they align with your intuition and the essence of your brand. This integration and embodiment ensures that your actions are purposeful and in alignment with your vision. By aligning your core values, passions, and purpose with your online presence and strategy, you establish a genuine connection with your audience, leading to greater trust and resonance.

Now that we have discussed the common blocks to embodiment and how to overcome them, here are a few practical tools to cultivate and embrace embodiment in your manifestation and entrepreneurial journey.

Live from the perspective of the future self you are manifesting. This technique of "living as if" is the full embodiment of the future self you know and love, the next-level-you in life and business, as if it has already manifested. This is very different and the exact opposite of "fake it 'til you make it!" This is the practice of BEING the next level you, feeling it, knowing it and owning it in every aspect of your life. Make decisions, take committed actions, and adopt habits that align with your future self. By doing so, you send a powerful message to the universe that you are ready to receive your manifestations. It is also the process of being honest with yourself and when you feel resistance or do not have faith at the moment. When this happens, be conscious of and recenter yourself, and boldly remind yourself who you know you are while embodying every aspect of it. It's natural to have doubts and uncertainties along your journey, but cultivating unwavering faith in yourself and the universe is crucial. Trust that the universe is always conspiring in your favor and that you have the skills and resources to manifest your dreams. Embrace the unknown and lean into the discomfort, knowing that every step you take is a step towards your desired outcome.

Visualize and embody what you desire. Close your eyes and vividly imagine that you are living as your future self, having already achieved your goals and desires. Embody the desired outcomes by envisioning not only the external achievements but also how it feels to accomplish them. Engage all your senses, visualize yourself taking inspired action, and imagine the emotions associated with achieving those goals. This practice anchors your desires within your physical experience, increasing their manifestation potential.

Journal and write about your future self, your business, or anything that you are creating as if you are already living that reality. Describe in detail how it feels, what you're doing, and the impact you're making. This exercise helps anchor your intentions in the present moment.

Be in a space of gratitude for what you have now in your physical reality and what you are manifesting. Gratitude shifts and elevates your energy, makes you more open and receptive to all that you desire and that the universe has to offer. Gratitude can be a practice in the evening to acknowledge the positivity in your day, in the morning to set the intention for what you are creating, or any time of day to reground and refocus yourself.

Embodiment plays a vital role in the success of your manifestation journey. By consciously integrating your thoughts, emotions, and actions with the physical experience of running an online business, creating a desired outcome in your life or up-leveling who you know yourself to be, you can authentically unlock your manifestation potential, and achieve remarkable success in all aspects of life and business.

Kim McGuire, MSN, RN is a business consultant, and a high performance mindset mentor, who has developed innovative programs for major hospital systems across the country, owned successful businesses and has taught energetics and healing techniques to clients all over the world! She is also a speaker and facilitator focusing on process improvement, personal and leadership growth and the power of beliefs and communication. Kim specializes in and is passionate about supporting leaders to elevate to their next level of personal and business success. She can be reached at kmcguirenurse@gmail.com.

CHAPTER 6

Perfectly Imperfect

by Dyan Moeller

There are many phases of our life, but one that we cannot escape is our childhood. Some of us had the most amazing childhood, others not so much. The tricky part is that the values and morals that are instilled in us come at an early age and are carried into adulthood. I used to think that no one had the childhood I did. As I got older, I realized that although that was true, we all had experiences that shape who we are and where we are going. Those experiences are some amazing lessons if we analyze them and see them as an opportunity. The best part about getting older is the maturity to realize that we are all here for a purpose. We may all be here to learn something different, but the overall goal is the same and that is for us to leave better than we came.

When I first met Kimberly, I knew she had the ability to make lemonade out of lemons. Why was she someone who was able to turn things in her life around, and how did she do it? We often look at people and compare our lives to theirs. We believe they hold some magical secret that allows them to pivot and change. As I became a student of

Kimberly's, the very first section in her coaching program was about mindset and limiting beliefs. Oh, the dreaded mindset - I was sure I didn't need that. How is that supposed to help me make money and be profitable? So, just like most of her other students, I skimmed past it and skipped to the next section. Time went by and not much changed for me. I had a million ideas and was very good at shifting from one thing to another. When I got bored, or when things didn't pan out, I would switch again. Restlessness and boredom seemed to come easily.

It wasn't until I was almost finished with my 12-month coaching program that I realized that perhaps I had overlooked a section as I didn't feel like things were coming together for me as I had hoped. I dug deep to figure out what it was that Kimberly had that I didn't. I was kind and funny, just like she was. So what was the magical secret she kept? Surely God must have given her some special asset that I didn't have.

As it turns out, there really was no magical secret. There was no reason why I couldn't be as successful as she was. She had already done the work that needed to be done, but what was it? Mindset and limiting beliefs! Did your eyes roll when I said that? You have thousands of daily opportunities from the time you get up to the time you go to bed. Sometimes, how we start our day off determines how our day will go. Ever hear someone say, "*I woke up on the wrong side of the bed,*" or "*I overslept and the rest of the day was a struggle?*" What we tell ourselves and how we treat ourselves truly matters.

What I noticed about Kimberly is that she actually loves herself, imperfections and all. She is able to laugh at herself when she makes a mistake, and she is able to pivot and try something new when things are not going as planned. She is determined to figure things out and is relentless about it. Now, did I say she was perfect or that she never makes a bad choice? Did I say she balances everything and it always works out the way she wants? Of course not. What you don't see is what's going on in her mind and how she is able to pivot from something that is not working to trying something else. What you don't see is the work that she has already done. She is just at a different place in her journey than you are.

Having limiting beliefs keeps you safe, keeps you "stuck." It also allows you to self-sabotage and give yourself an out. Telling yourself, "*It wasn't going to work out anyway,*" or "*I am just not like that,*" will allow you to sit as if on a merry-go-round that goes in circles, but never ends up anywhere. Think about what your limiting beliefs are about: Is it money? Is it a successful marriage, being a parent or helping the homeless? For each of us it can be very different. The most important thing is that the desire is there. But it takes pulling back layers and really looking at what it is that you want. If you are superficial, you will be superficially fulfilled. You can't get there if you don't know where you are going.

Here are five strategies to help.

Think of someone you want to be like and notice their attributes. How do they present themselves and what has gotten them to where they are? Do you believe they are successful? Now look at your own attributes. What does success mean to you? Success is not a straight up trajectory. It's more like a roller coaster going upside down, in the dark. It's up and down and turns on a dime. BUT the track is what keeps it going repeatedly. The track never stops, and you must not either. Pivot, maybe, but don't stop.

When you meet someone who you want to be more like, what you don't see is what they have been through to become that person. They are evolving and will continue to do so, but it's taken time. Kimberly has said repeatedly, "*I knew I wanted something different for my family.*" That was enough of a vision for her to start doing something different like live social media videos from her car. She was constantly making small changes where she could because she knew those changes would add up. She also worked on her mindset and self-sabotage. She will tell you, "*It was sometimes easier to fail because I knew it would push me forward.*" Why? Because she knew she deserved what she wanted just as much as anyone else.

So, I encourage you to listen quietly. What does the word "success" mean to you? How do you define it? Take out a piece of paper and start writing what your version of success means. Don't overthink it, just start jotting down what comes first.

Next, give yourself two gifts: the gift of time and the gift of forgiveness. Success will not happen overnight unless you define success as money and win the lottery the next day. Carrying extra guilt, shame, or imperfections is a huge, weighted suitcase that only drags you down. It serves zero purpose. The key to this is allowing and acknowledging that it's okay to make mistakes. The second key is to learn from those mistakes.

Third, keep what you want in your line of sight and hold fast to your vision. Imagine being on the highway. Change lanes if you must, but stay on it. As you go through your journey, there will be distractions along the way, or you may realize that what you wanted or what you previously thought determined success has now changed. That is the beautiful part of the journey. But you still have the drive to keep on pursuing. After that, share it with someone who means something to you.

Surely you have heard that birds of a feather flock together - it's true. Surround yourself with like-minded people who get you and support you. They are the ones who understand and will be there for you when you're questioning yourself. It can be more than one person; in fact, it's great to have more than one because you will be exposed to different perspectives, and some people might help you navigate situations that you come across better than others.

Lastly, start your day with gratitude. When you get up in the morning to start your daily routine, think of the things you are grateful for. If you can find gratitude in the simplest things, you set your day up for success and your day will be brighter. If a gratitude practice is new to you, you can start small - did you wake up this morning and the refrigerator was still running? Did the dog make it through the night without having an accident? Did your car start again this morning?

I wish I could tell my 20-year-old self all these things and learn a little earlier. But we all go through phases and stages of our lives at different times and we are forever learning. Give yourself some grace. You don't have to do anything perfectly; you just have to take the first step.

Dyan is Kimberly Olson's Executive Assistant and is very passionate about *Goal Digger Girl Co* as she has completed all of their programs and has become an integral part of the community. She lives in Denver with her husband of 30 years, has three kids and is a Pediatric Nurse.

CHAPTER 7

The Power of Wealth Acclimation

by Joanna Gard

Have you ever felt unworthy of something good coming into your life or found yourself sabotaging a great experience? I grew up in a home where both parents were alcoholics. My dad was constantly in and out of jobs and my mom worked her ass off to barely make ends meet. It was constant chaos, fighting, and so many times I felt like just another mouth to feed. I had so much financial insecurity as a child, constantly living with the fear of waking up and not having heat, water, food or a roof over our head. I was embarrassed because of my stained, shabby, ill-fitting clothes that smelled of cigarette smoke as I went to school. This was in stark contrast to the super rich people my mom worked for. She owned and operated her own cleaning and yard service business and she worked for heirs to Budweiser, families with Texas oil money, and the chancellor of the University of Denver. I watched as my mom gave so much of her time and attention to her clients so we could live in a double-wide trailer. She single-handedly put food on our table, a roof over our heads, and she clothed us and did everything else that it takes to run a household. Honestly, we never went without because of her hard work, perseverance, and determination.

Although we always had the physical necessities, what I wanted was my mom's attention and love. Because she worked so hard during the day, she had nothing left to give at the end. After work, I would watch her sit alone at the kitchen table and drink a beer and smoke a cigarette. I wanted so badly to sit with her and talk to her and tell her about what was going on in my life, but she needed space. My young mind interpreted this as: *I was unlovable and unworthy*. That space that she needed created a deep sense of unworthiness in me. The unworthiness that I felt became like a mental prison that I built for myself. I liken this unworthiness that I felt to a chain.

Do you know how they train huge, massive elephants not to leave the circus? When the elephant is just a baby, they tie a chain around its leg. No matter how hard she pulls and struggles, the baby isn't strong enough to break free from the chain. Because elephants have incredible memories, as she grows in size and strength, she still holds the belief that the chain is stronger than she is. Even given the size and strength of the elephant, she doesn't try to break free.

As I grew up, I would count myself out of trying new things because of this deep sense of unworthiness. I lived chained to unworthiness for a very long time, until the day that my sister invited me to a spiritual meeting. It was a gathering of people who believed God loves humanity and they would tell whoever walked through the door about this great Divine Love. The meeting was getting ready to wrap up and the man speaking up front said to me, in front of the whole crowd, *"Do you know that God loves you?"* and I was like, *"No!"* Remember the chain of unworthiness? There is no way that the God of the universe could love me. Doesn't he know who I am? But from this moment on, a piece of the chain was broken. I saw myself differently than I ever had before, and through a lot of self-development work, healing, meditation, prayer, and wise counsel, I began to see my own power, strength, and beauty. I realized I was like the big elephant who had the power to easily walk away and break this chain holding me captive. I began to see that I was worthy of good things in my life, worthy to live the life I dreamed of. I started healing this part of myself that felt unworthy and ashamed.

I've come to a place in my life where I give myself the opportunity to try new things and I no longer have this deep sense of unworthiness. One of the new things I've allowed myself to do is take this information I've learned and teach it to other people. Unfortunately, as I looked around, I saw many other people held back by their own chain of unworthiness and financial insecurities. I created a group coaching program where women were allowed to experience luxury, value, and worth. A place where they could acclimate to receive beauty, support, and love. Then I co-created and co-led *The Money Game*, which is a game for people who are ready to think about money differently. This happens through playing fun games that easily shift your mindset, healing old traumas, and acclimating and embodying a new version of themselves. Through this process, people begin to see themselves as worthy and wealthy and allows them to break through glass ceilings.

This healing journey is a process. It's not that I woke up one morning deciding that I felt worthy and financially secure, and magically every moment of my life has been spent in this worthiness and security. It's not like going to college and getting a degree. Rather, it's a daily practice - remembering who I am, that woman that God loves deeply. A big strong powerful elephant that has the power to easily break the chain of unworthiness and financial insecurity.

My daily practice consists of meditation and connecting with the divine, allowing myself to experience more love, more pleasure, more freedom. A part of healing the chain of financial insecurity has been developing a process to help others break free called *Wealth Acclimation*. It is the process of going from being a woman trapped by her past, chained to unworthiness and held captive by fear, to a woman who knows and steps into her full power. Wealth acclimation is the process of reclaiming my power. I believe we all get to define wealth on our terms. It might be a large house with a fancy car or it might be living in a tiny home and spending your time gardening or creating art.

You get to determine what a life of wealth means for you. For me, wealth is a both/and life. Both a beautiful home AND a home full of love and joy; both an amazing career AND plenty of time to spend with my kids, husband, family and friends. It is also feeling a deep sense of worthiness of these things; worthy of success, worthy of love, and worthy of the money that I earn and receive. We have to start feeling happy, healthy, and worthy NOW, so when the money comes we already have those feelings.

Wealth acclimation has three powerful processes: radical self-inquiry, unapologetic self-love and powerful presence.

The inner work of radical self-inquiry involves asking the hard questions, facing your deepest fears and knowing yourself intimately. This gives you the power to acclimate to the wealth and abundance you desire. Unapologetic self-love allows you to find meaning within yourself, rather than seeking it outside of you, and comes from a deep sense of knowing that you are valuable because you exist. This allows unworthiness to float gently and easily away because you love yourself deeply. Powerful presence allows you to live in this moment the way you want to be, in order to live your future moments the way you want to. Each of these steps helps break the chain that binds you, and allows you to step into the freedom you so desperately desire.

This is the piece that I've seen missing in both the financial strategies and self-development fields. You have to acclimate, become accustomed, and conditioned to new beliefs, new thoughts, and new actions in order to break the chain that holds you captive. Have you ever felt unworthy of something good coming into your life? Or have you ever found yourself pushing something good away because you felt undeserving of it? It's okay, you're not alone. You can break this chain and break out of the mental prison that keeps you from living all that you're meant to live. It starts right now- today, at this moment. You can see yourself as worthy of all good things and remind yourself of your power. You're like those big elephants and you can easily walk away from this chain that holds you back. Claim your wealth and ability to acclimate to wealth now. Let's be done with the chains and mental prison of unworthiness and financial insecurity and step into a life full of wealth, beauty and love. Let's take up as much space, be as loud as we want, and make as much money as we damn well please!

A self-made millionaire, and entrepreneur for over 15 years. Joanna supports women taking up as much space, being as loud and making as much money, as they damn well please! Joanna is a wife, and mama to two beautiful girls. She has created a lifestyle that is harmonious between work and home. She and her family live on a mini farm. They raise goats, Colorado Mountain dogs and there's usually some kind of baby animal to be found. Their favorite activities as a family are camping, stand up paddle boarding, rafting, reading and playing games.

CHAPTER 8

Rewire Your Brain for Success

by Dr. Sharon DeHope

Our mind has over 70,000 thoughts per day. That is astounding! It also is frightening when we realize that many of these thoughts are negative, putdowns, and generally unhelpful to our success in life. We have formed our basic ideas in life by age seven, and have learned them mostly from our family: *Don't touch the stove! Don't climb on the furniture! Don't go out in the street!*

The habits we base our existence on is not our fault, it just is. What we learn to do about this is in our control.

I was raised by a stay-at-home mom who was an alcoholic. This was not her fault and during the 1960's, when this was happening, women had no solutions for alcoholism. Parenting a parent and a younger sibling is not a recipe for a successful future. My Dad, however, was my hero, my rock, and tried to be both mother and father to us when he was home. Somehow, God kept alive in me a spark of pushing myself to achieve more for myself.

Boom! Life as I know it changed forever. Obsessive thoughts of doubt and worry hit me one day and didn't stop. Not having any idea of what was happening, I just kept pushing onward, willing it, and praying for it to stop!

What exactly is Obsessive Compulsive Disorder?

Thoughts come into your brain that are unwanted, but the more you try to stop them, the greater it has power over you. The compulsions are rituals that your brain tells you will stop the thoughts, so you have to do them in order to get some relief. My compulsion was hand washing and my obsession was seeing germs everywhere. This mental illness has been with me since 1986; it's part of me. I accept that today, and monitor its sneaky ways and my behavior.

The biggest mistake I made back when this started was not taking good care of my physical health. When we work ourselves to exhaustion, skip meals or get little sleep, our brains can fatigue. This brain fatigue leads to anxiety, depression and can result in you having a breakdown. With a proper diagnosis, therapy, and medication things improved for me. My life looked quite fulfilled from the outside: a loving husband, two beautiful children, and a Chiropractic practice at home.

As my kids grew older, we chose to move to the beach in New Jersey. I closed my practice and transitioned to staying home with my kids. It was then that I walked into my first network marketing party and was intrigued by the business. I discovered that my self-development journey was the missing part of my life.

I was still struggling with low self-esteem, low self-image and mental blocks. Yes, someone can look happy and successful and still feel like an impostor inside. The feeling of unworthiness was my biggest negative self-belief. I saw what others had and never thought I deserved the same. Even if I accomplished something, it never felt like it was enough.

These self-limiting thoughts and beliefs are very powerful and not easy to remove. First you have to do the work to recognize them. Next, you need the desire to remove them. It is not simple or easily accomplished just by taking a single action.

Our minds are very powerful and made up of both our conscious and unconscious parts. Simply wanting change is a starting point, but it must be followed by action. Repeating affirmations was an effective tool for me. I tried *Post-It* notes on my mirror and computer. Next, I found a *YouTube* video for morning I AM statements. I committed to listening to and repeating them every day for 21 days. I said those affirmations looking at myself in the mirror. Most of those statements I still say today in the shower. This is a very relaxed state of mind to be in, and is so effective in helping the affirmations to sink into your unconscious mind.

I continued to read powerful books, listen to podcasts, and joined a coaching program that worked on my subconscious thoughts. I also read about developing a morning routine that started setting me up to be more proactive in my day. I did the work and wrote down my two goals and repeated them throughout the day. Only about two percent of people actually write down their goals. Even less look at them daily or carry them around. Mine were taped to my bathroom mirror where I would see them every day.

I still needed more coaching and more messaging in my brain to finally decide that I deserved success in my life, and to feel worthy to go after the life I wanted. My life was wonderful these last few years, without me needing anything else for a comfortable life. But I wanted more from myself. I had finally tossed aside the negative self-talk, stopped putting myself down and was ready to begin manifesting the many goals that God was putting on my heart.

Successful people can have mental illnesses, low self-esteem, and low self-worth from their upbringing, from trauma or from poor decisions. I healed myself by educating myself about personal development, getting mental health treatment and by having a positive attitude that keeps me on a path of success. It happened for me and can happen to anyone willing to search, be relentless, study, persevere and have faith in God. My goals are to share what I have learned and to guide many other women to find themselves again.

Positive thoughts can become a new habit that reframes limiting self-beliefs. Starting by really listening to how you talk to yourself is step one. Next, change any negative dialog into positive words to say to yourself. Continue adding new habits that strengthen your belief in yourself. Find a mentor, a coach or program that really takes you through at least six months of transformation and accountability and that keeps you aligned with breaking down the negative talk in your subconscious. It is going to work if you do the work.

Remember it's never too late to go after your old dreams or find new ones. So many people went for their goals and dreams and were told no, repeatedly and they kept at it! The attitude that defeats self-limiting beliefs is that you are valuable, unique and filled with God-given talents that were given only to you. Your imagination can take you to the highest levels and then you need consistent action even when you feel like giving up. That's the real way to break through self-limitations. Change your mindset and your life will change.

Dr. Sharon DeHope is a Doctor of Chiropractic, turned Mindset and Business Coach for women who want to go after their old or new dreams. Delving into your self-image, reaching for goals that scare you, and resolving blocks holding you back are the foundation of her coaching. Sharon is also a serial entrepreneur, author, podcaster and teacher. Interviewing women to share their stories, successes and challenges are at the core of her podcast and work as a coach. As a wife to Paul, mom of two, grandma to Adelaide and Theodore, Sharon has a very busy life. The desire to help others has always been part of Sharon's day to day. Remember it's never too late to go after your dreams.

Part 3: Life Lessons that Last

Letting go and trusting God, ourselves, and that our dreams are worthwhile is probably one of the hardest challenges you'll face as an entrepreneur.

But what if we measured our faith in our ability to trust? We say we are faithful…but do our thoughts align with that? If not, do some reflection work and ask yourself why you don't trust.

Things will become magical when you truly realize that you are 100% responsible for your finances, your success and your happiness. You are.

Let's hear some life lessons that will inspire you to know that you can have anything you want in your life, and it starts with you.

CHAPTER 9

It's All in God's Timing

by Allyson Mancini

Your dreams happen in God's timing and sometimes success doesn't alway unfold the way YOU plan for it to or think it should. Usually life is nothing like what you thought it would look like. Yet you find you are exactly where you are supposed to be...if you allow it to happen and learn in the moments.

My early childhood was spent in a traditional conservative family; Mom and Dad, three girls, a dog, a two-story house, a country club membership and a *Cadillac*. The dream family... until it wasn't.

My parents divorced when I was 12 and life changed drastically. We went from a 3,000 square foot spacious home to an 800 square foot one-story home with one bathroom for three of us. I went from arriving home to fresh baked cookies to an empty house with little inside the pantry or fridge to eat. My mom went into survival mode, working a full-time job, a part-time job and attending college for the first time to get her associates degree at the age of 42.

Watching her, I decided then and there that I would rely on no man. In my eyes men were not dependable or trustworthy. I was determined to always be able to take care of myself and make my own money. No longer would I live in a state of lack, or limitation. I was going to be a successful career woman! That is, once I got through college.

As I said before, life has a funny way of making its own plans. My sophomore year in college I met Nick, and we pretty quickly knew that we wanted to spend the rest of our lives together. We graduated from a small business college in Northern Michigan, getting engaged the Christmas of our Senior year, and moved to South Florida in February of 1993. We were married by September. None of this was in my grand plan of being an independent, successful career woman. And now I was living far away from family and friends and married at the age of 22, trying to figure out adulting. By 1996 we had our son, Nicholas and 2.5 years later our daughter, Alexandra (Lexi).

I had a lot of trauma from growing up with a single mom. I must preface this by saying my mom did the best she could with the situation at hand. As an adult, I am grateful for the values my mom instilled in me. I wouldn't be where I am without her belief in me and dedication to do all she could to give my sisters and me the best she could. Yet, I was still traumatized by the "aloneness" and feeling of abandonment of my dad leaving and my mom working so much. So with that, I had agreed with Nick that I would do the "stay-at-home" mom thing at least until Lexi was in kindergarten. I didn't want my kids to feel traumatized as I had. Yes, I now know that was just a "story" I told myself.

Again, God or the Universe, however you like to refer to it, had different plans. A good friend recently told me once that you are put on this earth for a reason, to carry out a job, task, responsibility and almost always it is NOT what you plan! We have to remember, it is not YOUR plan ever. It is His plan and being obedient to that is sometimes the hardest part.

Allyson's plan of being an independent, successful career woman was still going to be on hold, much to my disagreement. My assigned task, besides that of a mom, was now that of caregiver, advocate, and the loudest voice for my daughter following some serious medical diagnoses. I soon discovered my job during this season of my life was to ensure that Lexi received all the best therapy, doctors, and care possible as we battled numerous medical diagnoses from the time she was nine months old. These experiences with her taught me so much; working with difficult people, speaking up for yourself, speaking up for those you love who are unable to, managing my time and numerous appointments and activities, and things always changing! And I was really good at it. I was really good at seeing all of the moving parts in one big picture and being able to make sense of them. This season in life also taught me the importance of taking care of myself, learning the importance of eating good food, and self-care, just to name a few things. These lessons learned with Lexi would be put to use when I got horribly sick myself, when she was deathly ill in high-school, when our son was in college dealing with atypical medical issues, and going through a world-wide pandemic!

I have held my fair share of part-time jobs throughout my life. I started babysitting at the age of 12 and had my first "real" job at 14. I even nannied during college. I am no stranger to work. Upon graduation from college with my degree in Marketing/Management, I became an Assistant Manager at *Structure* (the men's *Express* of the 90's). I then hopped around, working at the family business in underground construction in dispatching and admin work, as a *Mary Kay* Beauty Consultant, as a Leasing consultant at an apartment complex, the Assistant Nursery Director at our church, and a Teacher's Aide at my kiddos' school. From there I went into insurance for a property management company and then *Cabi* as a Fashion stylist, amongst other direct sales companies. To say I was trying to figure out what I was good at, my passions, and just where I belonged in my career was an understatement. I used to look at my numerous jobs as a weakness, but now I know they have been one of my greatest strengths! Through each one, I learned my skills that I am strongest at, and I now know that I was using them in each setting to be successful.

Then it happened. I believe this happens to us all at least once, if not more than once. There are events that change you to the depth of your soul...trauma that renders you a completely different person, causing you to look at the world through new lenses.

Three things happened in almost immediate succession in our world. Our daughter Lexi got deathly ill at the age of 17, we had a hurricane come through that potentially could have been catastrophic, and then a few months later our community was rocked by the shooting at *Marjory Stoneman Douglas High School* in Parkland, Florida. All of it mashed together and made me seriously question my purpose in this world. I knew I had to make changes, I just wasn't sure what they were. Life was short and unpredictable and I wanted to enjoy each moment as much as possible!

Going into March of 2018 I was at a loss and decided I needed to stop what I was doing and figure it out. So I resigned from being a *Cabi* stylist, which I was quite good at. I just decided to *be*, and thankfully my husband gave me the space to do just that. We had a lot coming up with Lexi graduating high school, Nick's parents' 50th wedding anniversary and our son, Nicholas, had spent his first year away at school in Connecticut.

So I took the time to be a mom. Focusing on all of the graduation events, Lexi's last year of competitive dance, and getting her ready to head off to school in Texas at *Baylor*. Along with supporting Nicholas in his transition of moving back to Florida and transferring to *UCF*, after career-ending injuries in hockey.

Remember I said all the lessons learned caregiving for Lexi would come back to be of enormous help for me and others? In 2019, during our first year of FULL empty-nesting, we found ourselves in uncharted territory with Nicholas. It was his turn to get my support and care with his health. Thankfully, this time around I was able to quickly assess and get him moving in a positive direction due to all of my past experiences.

After six months of medical leave from *UCF*, Nicholas returned to college in the Fall of 2019, and Lexi returned to *Baylor* for her sophomore year. About a week prior to Lexi going back, we went to visit a good friend at *Make-A-Wish* Southern Florida, an organization close to our hearts. Long story short, by the time we left, I had an offer to come interview for a position at *Make-A-Wish*! I thought I had *finally* found something that I felt passionate about and that was for me. My career was finally taking off!

Again, God had other plans. I love the mission of *Make-a-Wish* (MAW) and was honored to spend seven months working with some amazing people bringing love, joy and fun back into families' lives that I could so closely relate to. It was very healing for me. When the pandemic hit, within 48 hours, I lost my job at *MAW* with no plan to bring me back. During my time at *MAW* I had joined another direct sales company. It was very obvious at this point that I have always had the entrepreneurial bug!

Through training, I was introduced to this dark-haired beautiful, professional woman who was crushing it on social media and in direct sales, Kimberly Olson. Her energy was magnetic! I was intrigued and honestly impressed and decided pretty quickly that I had to learn from her. So, I jumped into one of her free challenges. I mean how awesome, she was offering free content, what?? Amazing! And then... she had a program, she had systems, she had strategy. She taught you how to use social media authentically in a way that didn't feel icky! I was sold, even before the beautiful box and shiny manual with the lessons!

We had a one-on-one coaching call, which I think was about two weeks into the pandemic. It was amazing! She could read me so well, and I knew my path was forever changed. Kimberly hired me as a Virtual Assistant, doing *Pinterest* and blog posts. Soon after I moved into numerous tasks that were client-related. I became the Community Relations Manager, which evolved into Human Resources. I now have the honor of being the Operations Director at *Goal Digger Girl Co* with a Goal to be COO (wink, wink ... manifestation at its finest).

I am 52 at the time of writing this chapter, and I am living my best life! And it keeps getting better. I love what I do here at *Goal Digger Girl Co.* I get to be the best version of myself, using my strengths every day to support the team and our clients. Never EVER would I have thought I would find my calling at the age of 50. I thought that time was past. I had resolved that my calling was being a stay-at-home mom and now that time was over. There are seasons in life for everything. Looking back, I can now see how my path was exactly what I needed. And my values, beliefs and innate skills have always been a running theme no matter what I have done. I am grateful for a CEO/Owner who is able to see the potential in everyone around her, including her team. I am grateful for her belief in me and her ability to let me continue to grow into the best version of myself!

I will continue to use my strengths to be the best I can for her, the team and our community until I can't physically do it anymore. NEVER give up, or think it is too late! It is never too late and you are never too old. And another thing I will never forget that she told me is that you only have to know about 10% more than those you are leading or teaching, so don't ever use the excuse of having too little experience or lacking a degree. Everything is figureoutable and you are a resourceful, badass boss babe! Now go CRUSH IT!

Allyson Mancini is the Operations Director at *Goal Digger Girl Co.* Allyson grew up a Michigander and now lives in South Florida. She earned her degree in Marketing/Management at *Northwood University.* She has been married to Nick for 29 years with two amazing adult children. Before coming on to *Goal Digger Girl Co.*, she was a SAHM/part-time worker for 24 years. Now an empty nester and full-time back in the work world, Allyson has discovered her true passion supporting and encouraging women in all aspects of their lives! All of Allyson's past work experiences have given her the deep desire to support, encourage and inspire women and she is honored to be a part of the *Goal Digger Girl* Headquarters!

CHAPTER 10

Creating a Leadership Lifestyle

by Trienne Topp

"I believe every woman has a leadership VOICE inside her calling to the next level to impact the lives of others. She feels called to serve, to mentor, make a difference, to guide starting with herself because a woman who can lead herself first, can lead others."

Trienne F. Topp

Twenty-six. That is how many years I have held leadership titles in my lifetime. Yes, I am lovingly going back to age 16 when I was the *Miss Michigan Pinto Princess;* the horse, not the car. At the same time, I was our 4-H club President, taking dance lessons two nights a week, working at a local restaurant as many hours as allowed, and successfully completing all my high school AP classes.

I shake my head now just thinking about it all. Somehow though, I do not recall feeling "under pressure" to succeed during those early years. I also don't recall anyone ever handing me a permission slip to be a teenage badass. I just did it. No questions asked, no imaginary ceiling or limitations, no big expectations set except that *I could*. I was leading myself without realizing how those choices would add up in the future.

If you look up *leadership* in Webster you get: *'the office or position of a leader, the capacity to lead, and the act or instance of leading'*. If you ask our friend Google (because if we don't ask Google is it really accurate?) we see *leadership* as: *'the action of leading a group of people or an organization'*

What about when we define *leadership* for ourselves? If no one else is coming to tell us what to think or do next - then what is leadership? To me, *leadership* is a way of being and making choices with integrity while positively influencing the people and world around us simply because we can. There is no one looking over our shoulder at this point telling us what is right and wrong, no one "should-ing" our every move, and no one but ourselves questioning our decisions. Afterall, a woman who can lead herself, can lead others.

With each career move through the restaurant industry, fashion retail, and network marketing, I always embodied that feeling of leadership, the example, the expected level of service. It wasn't taught and there was never one of those "ah-ha" moments that I noticed that I was creating a leadership lifestyle. Instead, I knew that it was important for me to take responsibility for my own decisions and actions. My mom always said to me, *"You are free to make your own choices, but you are not free of the consequences."* So thinking that every decision I made was going to create a result; a result leading me toward my goal or one keeping me from those same goals. Consequently, being a Leader in almost every aspect of my life was a necessity.

You can create a *Leadership Lifestyle* too. Tony Robbins shares that *"Life is happening for us, not to us."* With that in mind, we are offered many opportunities every day. We can either create the life we want for ourselves and our families, or we can succumb to the circumstances that fall at our feet. One of those choices shows drive, intention, and leadership. I'm sure at this point you can guess which one.

We can create our *Leadership Lifestyle* starting in one area of our life that we want to make an immediate impact, or we can use the generality of a **"Wheel of Life"** covering:

- Faith
- Fitness
- Family
- Finances

- Friends
- Fun
- Future

You see, either way is a choice. A choice to lead ourselves to create the lifestyle we dream and embody, or to give up and let life happen as it will without making intentional decisions. Making decisions from a place of leadership will not always be easy, but it will always be worth it. We start by taking each category and asking some thought-provoking questions.

Let's take a look at just one area for now, so that you can take quick, messy, leadership action.

FUTURE:

Cue the scene from *"The Notebook"* where Noah is asking Allie in a tone that we can all hear in our heads *"What do you want!? What do you want!?"* Nevermind if you are team Noah or team Lon. The point here is what about YOU? When you look ahead at your best-version future self:

1. What does my ideal day look like? How do I spend my time and energy? Where do I go? How do I contribute?

2. What do I want to be known for? Is the way I show up now contributing to that?

3. What could I do differently, starting today, to lead myself and my life towards the vision I have set?

Start by writing out your ideal day. Close your eyes and envision all the details from the time you awake to your night time routine. There will be times that you will stop yourself when doing this exercise and ask if what you are envisioning is even possible for you. Along with other authors in this fabulous book, we are going to continue to snap those limiting beliefs from our minds and our vocabularies. They are not serving you or your future self, and you deserve to be led well. Especially if you are the one doing the leading!

Secondly, ask yourself what you want to be known for? Are you expecting to be leading a company, a team, a household or even your personal brand? Each of those will look different in scope, but as we make decisions in each scenario they have one important thing in common. When making a decision, ask yourself if this will result in getting closer to what we want to be in our future, or will it get in our way? The ideas and actions that get us closer are the ones we confidently choose, standing in our belief in our own leadership and abilities.

Lastly, when we ask what we could be doing differently, we are open to real authentic answers. Leaders don't candy-coat or cover up the reality of situations. We look at our possible outcomes and choose confidently. YOU are the only one who can decide if that direction will keep you focused and on course to your vision or not.

Each of these answers will look different depending on your category and how big the gap is between the here/now and your vision. Leading yourself into that vision takes clarity, confidence, and the ability to trust in your own ideas. There are always areas that a coach, mentor, or accountability partner can be a resource for talking through options. However, at the end of the day YOU are creating your own life. The quality of that is determined by your ability to lead yourself in moment-to-moment decisions.

Oh, did we forget to talk about "those" moments? The ones where you question what you are doing and if you are really creating the life you envision. The moments that feel like your decision either way is not ideal, but you need to choose. Those will be the times that you will feel the least like a leader, but you will persevere as the leader. You are creating by doing the work. Every time you make a choice, you are building the confidence and strength in yourself as a leader others can trust, but most importantly as a leader that you, yourself, trust. When there isn't a clear path to a decision, take the time to listen to your intuition.

So go on…create your life with intention and share your service with the world no matter your title, position, or modality. The impact that you make along the way will far exceed the moments you question yourself and your abilities. Remember, true leadership starts with self-leadership. Together, we can create a world where women thrive as confident leaders in all areas of their lives. You were meant for a *Leadership Lifestyle* and you are the only one who gets to create that design.

Trienne is a no-nonsense Leadership Performance Coach, Trainer, Speaker, and Author with over 18 years in Restaurant and 8 years in Retail and Network Marketing. As a leadership coach, she is focused on business growth and building team leaders through developing leadership, culture, and exceptional service as the pillars to sustainable business/personal growth. She is inspired to work with women in all areas of leadership and personal development to help them confidently CREATE and BE the next-level versions of themselves.

CHAPTER 11

Getting into the Driver's Seat

by Jessica Perry

I vaguely remember my father telling me that if I wanted *Calvin Klein* jeans instead of *Levi's,* I would need to get a job. I was 14 when this conversation took place and the day after that is when I landed my first job. I called every store, restaurant and business in a two-mile radius in search of a place that would actually hire a 14-year-old. *Pudgie's* would. Yes, that is really the name of the fried chicken takeout restaurant that I walked two miles to every day after school. I was so pumped to be making money. And THIS was the start of my very unhealthy relationship with work and money.

After my *Pudgie's* days, I secured a job working in a professional photo shop 15 hours a week. I worked 40 hours in the summer while all my friends were at the beach, but it didn't bother me because I was making way more than the average wage and focused on making sure I went on the school trip to Paris. I have never been without a job since, and I lost any sense of a work-life balance for the next 24 years. I worked my way up the ladder in retail management during my 20's and 30's and was working 60+ hours a week, skipping meals, not taking care of my body and just letting work determine my life. I missed family parties, birthdays, trips with my friends and just having a "normal" weekend to rest and recuperate. Some holiday seasons I worked 15-hour days and one of my bosses even had the nerve to ask me one day why I left the store before closing if we didn't hit our sales goal! Not to mention that particular December I was working six- and seven-day weeks between my store and helping out another store.

I was so motivated by making money and because of the validation it gave me that I kept ignoring my own needs and desires. I became a slave to my job. The pressures of work often consume our time and energy, leaving us very little room for personal development and hobbies. The more hours you put in, the more productive and successful you are; that is the perception for most of us. When you aren't at work you are still stressing about work. Many of us find ourselves overworked and burned out, neglecting our personal needs and going through the motions in our own lives, instead of enjoying things that matter most.

One day I woke up and my heart just sank. Suddenly I felt like something was missing. For years I'd felt I was meant for more and that I wasn't living up to my potential. It finally hit me that this was the life I was now stuck in because of the decisions I'd previously made, and for allowing myself to get comfortable (aka complacent) in my situation. Change my circumstances now, after accruing debt and not having a savings account?! I was convinced that it would be impossible to change my circumstances because I didn't have enough money to scale back hours at work and go back to school, or to get a different job because who wants someone with only retail experience for a corporate position? Besides, if I did get a corporate position, surely I'd be making a lot less money and have to start as the low man on the totem pole.

Things only got worse after I met my husband and started a family because now I had a lot more responsibilities. While I wouldn't change any of those decisions, I did start to feel resentful because now *that* was holding me back. It was always something, just my luck I guess. That is what I truly believed. Until one day my world was altered forever. March 2020 was when my company made the tough decision to close down for a few months at the start of the pandemic. It was a scary time for everyone. For me, it was even scarier because I was laid off for the first time ever. I was 38 with a five-month-old and a 14-year-old, without a job for the first time in over 24 years. My mind started racing. What would I do, how would I make money to live? What was going to happen to my family? Not to mention, it killed my work streak of 24 straight years!

The day after "D-Day," I woke up feeling surprisingly relieved. I was forced to take off work for an indefinite amount of time, and my fate was not up to me, but up to chance. For once I had ZERO control over my situation and I finally embraced letting go of things I can't control. I won't go into the crazy details of the few months off that I had before being asked to be hired back and having to turn it down because my kids still had no care. Again, secretly relieved yet excited. I had been asked to join a network marketing venture by my friend for the umpteenth time and I had finally given in and said yes. Because I can't NOT make money, right?

I got a taste of what it was like to have my own business and work from wherever I wanted to, setting my own hours, on my own terms. I decided I wanted to really tap into how to do this successfully, because the way I was being taught felt kinda icky. So I found a mentor and would watch every day on *YouTube* on my rides around town getting the baby to nap. I fell in love with being my own boss not only of work, but of my life. I started eating healthier, focusing on taking better care of my body and getting my hands on as much self-development as I could (podcasts, books, audiobooks, you name it!). I realized that this was my second chance to live my life the way I wanted to, and to see if I could change my circumstances once and for all. I now felt the confidence and fire burning inside of me once again. Before this journey, I was the most cynical non-believer in the "power of the mind" nonsense motivational speakers had been spewing. Surely this "*if you want to be happy, just decide to be*" mentality was b.s. that only crunchy granola moms preached. And I mean no offense to anyone, it was a misconception I had during a time where I was angry at the world, and thought it was everyone else's fault that I was stuck in life.

I completely believe this was divine intervention and God had a greater plan for me. It was becoming clearer by the day as I allowed myself to be open to the possibilities. I became happier and more forgiving of myself. I spent the next three years developing new skills, adopting a growth mindset and soaking up as much information on my craft as I could. I took full responsibility for my life, my actions and my thoughts. I felt like such a powerful badass and was starting to show the world who I was. I came to realize that my mission and purpose in this life is to empower other women to cut the shackles off and expand beyond their perceived limitations.

I now am a certified high performance life coach and I teach women who are struggling to find the balance between work and life. If you're reading this, I know you're probably burnt out and exhausted all the time. I know you're so overwhelmed by the chaos going on around you. You're tired of constantly having to be productive, serving people at work and then coming home to serve your family and clean the house and do all the things. I know you're probably stressed out more often than not and definitely not taking care of yourself the way you should be, both physically and mentally. I want to share my expertise in high performance with you to give you insight on how to turn your burnout to Brilliance. Here are some of the invaluable pieces of advice I can give you:

1. **Mindset, mindset, mindset.** Make sure you spend time daily on self-development like journaling, listening to podcasts, meditating, reading. Fill your mind with positive energy and release any bad energy you are holding onto.

2. **Plan ahead.** Schedule out your days and weeks ahead of time - what work tasks you have, personal appointments,

driving time, everything! Being super organized and intentional with your time is key to feeling less chaotic and overwhelmed. I guarantee you will find more time in your schedule by nailing this piece. Meal planning/prepping fits perfectly here because you would be surprised at how much time that saves.

3. **Celebrate small wins.** Give yourself a reward for hitting goals, even if it's just that you've stayed positive and focused seven days in a row. Get used to being your own best cheerleader.

4. **Set priorities and boundaries.** Knowing your limits is important to keeping you working efficiently. It allows you to set your own hours of operation and expectations of your boss, your clients, your family and friends. You deserve respect, and your time and energy is valuable.

5. **Be present.** No matter what you're doing throughout the day, make sure you're in the moment and not thinking about things that have already happened or possible future events. Ancient Chinese philosopher Lao Tzu said *"If you are depressed you are living in the past. If you are anxious you are living in the future. If you are at peace you are living in the present."*

6. **Learn how to say no without feeling guilty or second guessing yourself.** Don't do things that don't serve you. I'm not telling you to be selfish, I'm just saying if you don't want to do something, then don't. Doing things out of obligation isn't fun for anyone involved. Conserve your energy and protect your peace, at all times.

7. **It's okay to remove people from your life.** If someone in your life has toxic energy and you just know they drain your spirit, stop allowing them into your space. You get to decide which actors play a part in your movie!

8. **Hang out with yourself.** Be still and reflect because self-awareness is everything. If you know your triggers, what motivates you, what prompts you to feel a certain way in specific situations, you can work on changing those behaviors instead of getting stuck in those feelings.

9. **Stop the excuses and self-sabotage.** This one is pretty self-explanatory, but if you read #8, you will learn to identify self-sabotaging behavior immediately and squash it.

10. **Trust yourself and be consistent.** Keep your head up no matter how hard it seems. Things will always work out for you if you focus on each failure as lessons, and experiences as stepping stones to you living the

extraordinary life you envision. Whatever you do, don't quit. You were brought into this life to achieve greatness, leave your footprint on the world and live a truly abundant life. Now go do it. XOXO, Jessica

Jessica Perry is a highly experienced and skilled high performance coach. With a background in sales management and a passion for health and wellness, Jessica is dedicated to empowering women to live their healthiest and most fulfilling lives. Through her coaching, Jessica helps women to maximize productivity while minimizing stress, so they can find clarity and purpose while reaching their highest potential. She draws on a wide range of tools and techniques, including mindfulness, goal-setting, time management, and stress-reduction strategies, to help her clients overcome obstacles and achieve their goals. With a warm and empathetic approach, Jessica provides personalized coaching that is tailored to each woman's unique needs. Whether you're looking to boost your career, improve your health and wellness, or find greater fulfillment in your personal life, Jessica is committed to helping you unlock your full potential and live your best life.

CHAPTER 12

Overcoming Imposter Syndrome

by Becky Lafave

You are kick a$$! That's right, you my friend get to own it!

My journey didn't start out as a business coach, rather, just the opposite. I like to say I was born an entrepreneur and developed it over time because I love money. It's true that I love money. When I was seven I had my first lemonade stand. At the age of 11 I sold candy at school during recess time and I also had my own newspaper route. Then I discovered at the age of 12 that I had a gift that needed to be developed as all my girlfriends would ask *"Can you cut my hair next?"*

Not knowing what the heck I was doing started my journey to becoming a hairstylist. Yes, you heard me, I had no idea - I just did it anyway and figured it out. Fast forward 32 years later, I've created and developed a mindset that helped me overcome this imposter syndrome that I was hanging on to that I wasn't good enough or smart enough to have what others had.

Let me explain what that means. All these years as a very successful hairstylist, growing my business, my clients would tell me, *"You would be a great coach."* While they were in my chair I was their mentor, cheerleader, and also psychiatrist. LOL. So I decided to venture out and start a coaching business. But the road to this is harder than I thought and I knew I needed some kind of training just to turn on a computer (true story, lol). My first big investment in myself and business was a mastermind class that cost more than my first car. While learning how to build a website, my client that I had been doing her hair for the past 20 years volunteered to edit it. I thought that would be great, until she said, *"Wow, Becky, you're dyslexic."* In a loving way, I should add.

I wasn't even sure what that even meant. I had never heard that word before. As she explained to me that I was not very good at spelling or writing, I laughed and thought, *"No Shit!"* At the time I was 41 years old and being told that rocked my world. My first thought was that that must be why I chose a career that was more on my creative side.

Now, I've always been a very confident and courageous woman in everything I've done, but in that moment when she innocently labeled me, this overwhelming feeling of imposter syndrome came over me and robbed me of my confidence. I felt like an impostor from all the success that I had achieved. I should say this was not her intent, but this is how our brains work. We need to be very aware of our own thoughts.

Next, I found myself starting to self-sabotage and doubt everything that I was doing. I even stopped building the website and thought maybe I shouldn't be a coach at all because everyone would think I was a fraud since I am dyslexic. I even went down the path of depression, creating anxiety from it all until it started to rob me of my own health.

Thankfully, Robert, my husband of 33 years, has always supported my journey, reminding me that I have always been that successful person no matter what somebody has labeled me. That was a big reminder for me that it does really matter *who* we listen to and hang out with on a daily basis as they can and will rob you of your dreams if we allow them to.

That's when I made a decision to show up every day for the woman that didn't believe in herself, who was labeled and wanted something more in her life. The woman who was feeling like an imposter but had all this purpose inside and just needed the support and guidance to show her the way. Throughout my career as a hairstylist, the one thing I love the most was helping women feel and look their best from the inside out.

One day, one of my clients introduced me to Network Marketing, and I started to transform even more. I thought this would be a great way to help more women become independent, confident and have their own business. That's when my leadership skills started developing even more; coaching women to build a business, learning time management, and showing up and learning social media marketing while rebuilding an even stronger version of myself. It's so important to always invest in yourself and in your business growth.

Overcome Imposter Syndrome and KICK A$$

I always felt deep down that I wasn't good enough; that was the imposter syndrome kicking in. But now I know that was the mean girl in my head telling me these things. The outside world would have had no clue that this was happening, and I worked even harder to overcome what was happening inside. I was feeling unworthy and like I had a secret that people didn't know because I was really good at hiding my dyslexia.

When we are labeled, it is a double-edged sword. You have this feeling of relief, but at the same time it can have a spiraling effect on how we feel about and how we view ourselves. It's like we carry it around like a badge without honor, and it can create a victim mentality that you begin to own. If you're not careful, it will rob you of a decade of your life like it did for me. It makes me think about all the other women going through a similar situation that I could have supported all those years. Being labeled can cause you to experience anxiety or depression. These are real things that are happening inside of us, it just doesn't have to define who we are or how we want to show up in the world.

I talk to other women that have gone through this, and they have said that they feel like it has given them an excuse to not show up or even want to move forward in their life. If you allow this label to make you feel shame, it will slow you down.

What you choose to focus on becomes your reality

You are so much more than the label that someone gave you. You have big dreams to make happen, so it may be a little harder at times but that's okay. It just makes for a bigger and better story when you get to tell yours.

So let's get rid of the stories. Let's get rid of the labels that make you feel like an imposter. Once you know what the mean girl voices are, you can slay them. When I get in a place where I start to worry or feel like an impostor, I know the mean girl is coming out, and it all starts with inner chatter. Yeah we all know her: she starts to list off all the things you can't do, or that you should do, or asks you *"Who do you think you are to _____?"* Start to journal and ask yourself what you're getting from these old limiting beliefs. Define them so you can slay them by replacing those feelings with what you really want to be able to move forward.

When I was saying yes to writing this chapter, I really questioned myself. Can I really do this? Can I be an author? I knew deep down I *had* to do this. I hope by reading this that it will help you to create more in your life.

Both Mel Robbins and Tony Robbins have a technique they use to move them from a scarcity state of mind to a peak one. I came up with my own, and I encourage you to do the same or you can use mine if it feels good to you.

So mine goes like this. I first ask myself this question: does this move me forward in the direction I desire in my life? If the answer is a *"Hellzz Yes,"* I learned to get out of my own way by clapping my hands and moving one arm in a forward motion at the same time saying *"f*** it, do it anyway Becky, f*** it, do it anyway Becky, f*** it, do it anyway Becky"*…screaming it at the top of my lungs, three times. Sounds crazy, I know, but it works.

You can imagine what your body and mind is doing at that moment, right? Well try it right now so you know how it feels when this happens to you. So, how do you feel? Amazing right! It is sending these little fire-slaying lightning bolts through your whole body and giving you permission to kick a$$, Sista, in your life.

This has truly helped me go to the next level in life and in my business. That was when I started to live by my personal brand, *She's In Charge Of Business.* When you see me on social media or speaking at conferences, I want to hear you say *"I am in charge of my business, Becky."* That is exactly how you can make big moves in your life. I can't wait to hear all about your success.

Today I am proud to say I have spoken on stages in front of thousands of women; I teach women every day on social media how to use social media marketing to build their personal brand, and I work with students all over the world in building their businesses. I am so grateful for all of the life lessons so far and hope to keep inspiring more women to recognize their own greatness. Give yourself permission regardless of what anybody else thinks or believes is possible. Do not deny yourself the life you want to live and yes, this includes the money you will make doing what you love. You are powerful. You are surrounded by miracles. You can have it all. You are in charge!

Becky Lafave is the creator of *She's In Charge of Business*, a multi-dimensional brand that serves female entrepreneurs through coaching programs, focused workshops and a whole lot of training on how to build successfully on social media. She's owned a successful business for the last

33 years, and is currently helping female entrepreneurs build a thriving business on social media. She has shared the stage with Ray Higdon and Kate McShea at *Rise to Freedom* events. She is a busy mom of two and lives in Gilbert, Arizona with her husband Robert.

Part 4: Casting a New Vision for Your Life

Vision doesn't come naturally to everyone, but I believe it is essential for lasting change. The subconscious mind operates and resonates with images, shapes, sounds, feelings…all things we can really tap into with vision.

It's easy to notice what we don't want, but quite another to get clear on what we *really* want. We are wired to complain about the weather, traffic and taxes…it's no wonder we have a hard time focusing on what we do want.

In order for you to change, you need a new roadmap. I personally love vision boards, vision movies or listening to present-tense affirmations recorded by me of what I'm calling into my life.

Start small and build upon the new vision for your life.

CHAPTER 13

The Power of Daydreaming

by Rebecca Pruett

Were you ever accused of being a daydreamer? Did you ever escape to a world where you could pick and choose your environment and your actions? The first time I discovered the wonder of daydreams was when I was 10 years old. I was supposed to be asleep and was angry that some adult thought I should be sleeping. I wanted to be someplace else. I wanted someone to notice me, and believe that I was important and worth something to someone. Most of all, I wanted to be less awkward and admired for my abilities. So I dreamt about situations as if everything had fallen into place. In my dreams I spoke intelligently and people were impressed, they noticed my confidence and how I could do anything I set my mind to do.

My real life was not nearly as pleasant and wonderful, and I escaped to my imaginary world every chance I got. But gradually, I developed skills and abilities and slowly left my imaginary world to build a real life. I made my escape into a world where I learned and built skills and strengths that would make employers want to hire me. I became respected and appreciated. I got married and had children. And then something happened. I kept growing, but I was just not satisfied. I really did not know what was wrong. I became restless again and found myself escaping back into the imaginary world. There, I discovered that the imaginary world was a place where I could reach for goals that everyone else said were impossible. I felt good again. I had power and direction in my dreams, and I could do the impossible.

At that moment, I remembered that I used to dream all the time. I used to escape into my daydreams, but now I have options that I did not have as a child. I have already figured out how to reach for dreams and make them a reality! Being a daydreamer tells me that there is still more for me to reach. This was the key. Things are impossible until you dream. That fantasy helps you imagine something bigger, something better.

What do you dream about? What is something you want so badly that you escape to that mental oasis when you feel trapped? It does not matter how foolish your dream is. Lately, in my discontent, my fantasy is to be like an eagle ... to escape from the nonsense and fly far above problems and glide on to my goal. Am I really going to be an eagle? Of course not! But this image points me toward a dissatisfied element in me and gives me a hint that subconsciously, I am looking for something more, something higher than what I currently possess.

All the imagining in the world is useless unless you do something about it. The true value of dreams is that they give you a true picture of what it is that you value. Look at your deepest dreams and fantasies. What does this tell you about your personality? If my greatest dream is to own a house on the beach, my picture of the beach will tell you what my desires are. If I picture a peaceful beach that extends as far as the eye can see with smooth rippling sand and birds in the air and a dolphin swimming toward me, a big part of my dream is a sense of peace, a sense of connection to the world, a sense of belonging, the need for a peaceful environment.

If my dream of a house on the beach is of the wildest party you've ever seen with fireworks and exciting people and scintillating interaction over alcoholic drinks, then my beach dream is about excitement and action and fun and as many people around as possible. Both images are on the beach, but what those dreams symbolize is widely different.

When I began my own business, I was in the middle of chaos, and I thought I wanted a beautiful home, a peaceful haven from the chaos. As I attained that goal, my home became more peaceful, but I found that this was not enough. I needed a sense of challenge, a problem to solve, a place to focus my energy, a focus so sharp that I could not see any other problems. In fact, peace is vital...but it is boring! I need peace so that I can focus. I need more than peace - I need it in my life so that I can focus my energy on solving a problem. When my home was chaotic, I had something to fight for. But when the fight was over, I was lost. I needed a new thing to fight for; a new challenge to conquer.

For most people, dreams are more than objects to acquire. They point you to something more, something you are missing. Do you want more positivity around you? Do you want to have the money to easily pay bills or to allow you to travel? Do you want to meet people and be surprised by them? You might be dreaming of tangible objects, but deep below those tangible objects, most people fantasize about intangible things, things that are difficult to put into words. That dream helps you look past the tangible toward what you really long for. The tangible is good, but most of the time, it is really a symbol of something deeper, something more.

In my business, I encourage people to create goal posters, to put their dreams where they can see them. Frequently people have tangible dreams of cars, houses, or vacations but miss the intangible dreams of impressing their father, or living a life of joy, or feeling fulfilled. That result is much more difficult to put your finger on and is harder to identify. So a tangible item is a great start to your goal poster. And then, when you reach that goal, consider why that tangible item was important. Ask yourself what it represents to you and why that is important.

One of the greatest gifts I have received in my business is the gift of self-discovery; the gift of discovering what is most important to me. As you look at your dreams, what do they say about you? What do they say about what you value? What do they say about what you want out of life? The fact that you picked up this book indicates you want more, that there is something missing in your life. You are the only one who can reach for those goals….who can reach out and grab them. You are the only one who can look at your fantasies, then evaluate your own skill sets, find the training needed and the people to help you make your dreams come true!

So how do you implement your dream? This starts with awareness of your dream. Do you wonder if you have a dream? Many people bury their desires so deeply that they believe they don't have a dream! But those dreams are still there. Your desires peek their heads out periodically, leaving you with a feeling of discontent or longing. This is a great sign! Next time that happens, stop and observe your feelings. Ask yourself *"Why?" "What triggered this?" "What do I really want?"* This unhappiness and discontent points you toward something missing in your life. Rather than bury it, pull that discontent out and look at it. If this was being described and experienced by someone else, what conclusions could you draw? Look back at yourself. Are those conclusions accurate? Now look at what fills that discontent, that gap between where you are and where you want to be.

What fills that need for you? Do you need people to really see you? What would make you feel seen? Do you need to be able to pay for your children's swim lessons or medical care? What could you do to make that money? Do you hate sending your children to daycare? What could you do so it would be unnecessary? Do you feel like you can't survive at home with toddlers without adult conversations? What could you do to adjust your situation so you have adult conversations? This is not a cookie cutter solution. This is something only you can solve for your particular situation.

What works for me might not work for you. However, this is where a business has power.

Being an entrepreneur enables you to customize your solution to achieve your dreams. Whether you need to make a little or a lot of money, you can find a business where you can do this! Anyone can build a business if they are willing to step out of the box of other people's expectations and reach for the dreams that are deep within them. Business is the place where we can discover our true potential and carve out our place in the world no matter what circumstances we were born into. We live in a world full of possibility and just need to find how we can contribute to this exciting place to build our own kingdom!

Growing up in an entrepreneurial home, Rebecca Pruett has a creative perspective on growing a business. That perspective has been enhanced by many years in a business law office, where she saw businesses start, fail, succeed, and thrive, and was further enhanced by the growth of her own business, in which she helps women build confidence and professionalism through skincare and makeup. Rebecca is excited to share that creative, business perspective and build up others as they discover the joy of business!

CHAPTER 14

Rooted in Faith

by Dr. Amy Nussbaum

When I was 26, I moved from Illinois to North Carolina. My parents questioned if this was truly necessary. I was single, didn't have a job, moving into an apartment I hadn't seen, all because of a calling God had placed on my life.

I had been serving in the music ministry for several years after graduating with my BS in Music; conducting choirs, leading praise teams, directing cantatas and musicals. God had different plans… I felt called to pastor. I loved preaching and teaching. Seeing lightbulbs of understanding in a congregant's eyes fanned the flame within me. After prayer and seeking counsel from several mentors, I applied and was accepted into a dual-degree program at a seminary in Charlotte, North Carolina.

I would be earning my Master of Divinity and my Master of Arts in Christian Counseling. I wanted to be as prepared as possible to serve God's people. My parents helped me move into my apartment on a Friday morning, I met with my advisor Friday afternoon, and New Student Orientation was Saturday. It was a whirlwind, but it was exciting. But something happened during one of our orientation sessions that has stuck with me all these years later. One of our counseling professors challenged us to consider, would we become a Christian Counselor or a Counselor who happened to be a Christian. At the time, I didn't understand the difference. However, as I continued my studies over the next few years, I came to understand the nuances between the two and how important it is to decide what role your faith will play in your career. With each shift I have had through the years, I have had to consider these same questions. And now, as you build your business, it's your turn.

What role will your faith play? Will your business be a faith-based business, or will you be a person of faith who happens to own a business? Let me encourage you to begin your consideration with prayer. You see, both answers are acceptable and God honoring. Psalm 32:8 says, *"I will instruct you and teach you in the way you should go; I will counsel you with my eye upon you."* (ESV). Seek God and he will give guidance. As you make this decision, you will want to choose a Scripture or two to become part of the foundation of your business. If you are choosing to build a faith-based business, these Scriptures may be used in your vision or values statement. Here are a few to get you started:

"You shall remember the Lord your God, for it is he who gives you power to get wealth, that he may confirm his covenant that he swore to your fathers, as it is this day." (Deuteronomy 8:18, ESV).

"Honor the Lord with your wealth and with the firstfruits of all your produce; then your barns will be filled with plenty, and your vats will be bursting with wine." (Proverbs 3:9-10, ESV).

"Now there are varieties of gifts, but the same Spirit; and there are varieties of service, but the same Lord; and there are varieties of activities, but it is the same God who empowers them all in everyone. To each is given the manifestation of the Spirit for the common good." (1 Corinthians 12:4-7, ESV).

"Whatever you do, work heartily, as for the Lord and not for men, knowing that from the Lord you will receive the inheritance as your reward. You are serving the Lord Christ." (Colossians 3:23-24, ESV).

As you begin drafting your mission, vision, and values statement, in addition to Scripture, you will want to reflect on how being faith-based will influence every area of your business. How you hire, who you will work with, what projects you will accept, and how you will manage and invest your money.

• Will you only hire like-minded individuals? Do you envision starting all your meetings with prayer? Or are you willing to employ those with a different worldview, hiring those with different faiths and beliefs than you, including those with no faith at all?

• Will you only accept clients who also have a foundation of faith? Maybe one of your foundation Scriptures is 2 Corinthians 6:14, *"Do not be unequally yoked with unbelievers. For what partnership has righteousness with lawlessness? Or what fellowship has light with darkness?"* (ESV). Or will you utilize your business to serve the world and introduce others to Christian principles?

• Will you only work on projects that encourage Biblical principles or are all projects viable options for you because they create income?

• Will you tithe your business income or possibly start a non-profit of your own to continue to serve your community? Or maybe you will implement a profit-sharing policy so all employees see financial benefit in addition to their salary.

Every area of your business needs to be considered through a biblical worldview when you are starting and running a faith-based business. For me, I chose to be a counselor, and now a coach, who is a Christian. It allows me to work with all kinds of people in all stages of life. Oftentimes, clients don't realize that I am giving them Biblical counsel, but I do utilize principles found in Scripture to guide my sessions. When I do have a client who shares my faith, when appropriate, I often offer to pray with them and even assign Bible readings for homework and reflection.

My faith infiltrates every area of my life, my thoughts, and my actions. I can give this gift to those I work with, sharing the love of Jesus with them, even if they don't realize it. I'm praying for you as you journey this path. It isn't easy. Living a Christian life goes against the grain of our culture. Running a faith-based business does the same. You may be asked to do something unethical, to look the other way or offer a questionable favor. Following God's path may turn others against you, but I promise, God's blessings will soon follow.

"Therefore take up the whole armor of God, that you may be able to withstand in the evil day, and having done all, to

stand firm." (Ephesians 6:13, ESV). - Rev. Dr. Amy LP Nussbaum

Dr. Amy LP Nussbaum is an ordained minister and life coach from Central Illinois. Amy thrives on building belief in women who are ready to rediscover their passion by revitalizing themselves. She has a Master of Divinity and a Master of Arts in Christian Counseling from *Gordon-Conwell Theological Seminary* and a Doctorate in Ministry from *Talbot School of Theology, Biola University*. After serving in prison ministry and hospital chaplaincy, she has served several churches, filling Associate and Senior Pastor roles. Amy's passion to preach, teach, coach, and mentor has led to her love of coaching.

CHAPTER 15

Small Steps, Big Wins

by Trisha Langford

Success is not a destination; it is a journey.

Winning in your goals requires a growth mindset, believing that you can learn and improve. It requires overcoming limiting beliefs and casting away those old beliefs that are holding you back. And taking action is required to be able to overcome those limiting beliefs. The action steps help to build confidence, develop new skills and challenge negative beliefs!

When setting goals, be specific about what you want to achieve in your goal, develop a timeline and milestones that will help you stay on track in achieving the goal. It is also important to be flexible and adaptable in your progress as unexpected challenges or opportunities may arise along the way.

To stay motivated and focused it is important to remind yourself of your goals and celebrate the wins along the way. Success can be a challenging and daunting process. It is important to celebrate every small win along the way to provide a sense of accomplishment and satisfaction which can help motivate one to continue to work towards our goals. At times we often get laser focused on the pursuit of the end goal, we overlook the progress we have made. This motivation can be especially important when setbacks take place along the journey.

Taking the time to slow down and appreciate life allows us to acknowledge and appreciate the progress we are making along the way, and it helps us to stay motivated for the end goal. In our lives and even more today than ever before we tend to focus on negativity and overlook the positives. We dwell on what we should have done, on our failures and look at our shortcomings. We tend to overlook the successes we have already achieved and continue to achieve every day.

Celebrating wins can positively impact our lives by reducing stress, increasing happiness and improving relationships. Celebrating the WINS is a way to acknowledge and appreciate the hard work and dedication that went in achieving a goal. It does not have to be complicated; it can be as simple as recognizing and acknowledging the win, big or small. By sharing it with others it can have an enormous impact on our lives, it helps to build confidence, our self-esteem, boost our mood and enjoy the journey. Small wins matter! How can we celebrate the small wins? It can be as simple as taking a moment to reflect on what we have accomplished. Achieving a big win is an incredible feeling of accomplishment and we get the warm and fuzzy feeling within us. It is that proud moment. Take the time to FEEL the excitement. Once the initial excitement wears off it can be hard to know how to savor that success. Here are tips on celebrating the small and big wins!

1. Start with keeping a gratitude journal and writing down your accomplishments, no matter how small they may seem. This will help you to reflect on your progress and appreciate the small wins and an opportunity to come and revisit the journey.

2. Share your wins. Share your wins with your family, friends, or your colleagues. This will not only help you feel good about your progress by reminding you where you have come from, but it will also inspire others to celebrate their own wins.

3. Treat yourself by rewarding yourself for all the challenging work you have been achieving. It does not have to be anything big, it can be as simple as giving yourself permission to take a break or go for a walk or do something

you enjoy. This will help you fill up your own cup and come back even stronger.

4. Set new goals. Celebrating your wins can be a great motivator in setting new goals. Use accomplishments as a stepping stone for a new challenge. Remember celebrating the small wins is not about feeling good in the moment, it is about building momentum. Enjoy the journey and celebrate the progress.

5. Take time to reflect on your journey and really FEEL the accomplishment. Think about how it makes you feel deep down inside, think about the challenges you have faced, the lessons you have learned, the people that have supported you along the way.

6. Capture the moment. Take photos to remember the details to share with others and for you to remember how you felt when you accomplished your goal. When we celebrate the big wins, we are more likely to continue to strive for success.

7. Share your success with others. When we celebrate big wins with others, we are more likely to continue to strive for success.

8. Give yourself permission to relish in the moment, take a deep breath in and take it all in; you earned it. You achieved that goal.

Overcoming any limiting belief is essential for personal growth and success. By identifying and challenging negative beliefs, seeking out positive role models and support networks, and taking action, individuals can overcome the self-imposed barriers they have set upon themselves and achieve their full potential. Winning and celebrating go hand in hand. Celebrating the winning is an essential part of the process and it provides the opportunity to acknowledge the progress and effort that has been put in. It reinforces one's beliefs in their own abilities and allows for reflection and closure of the goal or project. Acknowledge the hard work that went in, FEEL the success, and celebrate the WIN, big and small!!

Trisha Langford grew up in Montana, is a wife and mom of a blended family of six children and Glam-Ma to seven beautiful grand babies. She has a BSBA and works as a staff accountant, owns two beauty businesses in the digital space; a clothing boutique, and one health and wellness. She is an avid outdoors person that loves the mountains, the fresh air, hiking and being adventurous. She's building her dream home alongside her husband and living her best life! She is an inspiration to others, and has been able to serve others through her work.

CHAPTER 16

Leading Yourself First

by Mary Kate Berry

As a public figure, life is always challenging. When you are constantly in the spotlight in a small town, and your husband is mayor, you should assume drama is always nearby. And oh boy, that is precisely what happened when we got together, and I offered to take a position until they could fill it. My life was forever changed by the events of that night. It led to so much hurt and a feeling of betrayal from a few "very close friends." I worked to get past it, but being surrounded by the same people didn't help. So, now is the time to tell my story. From being a total hermit, because I was terrified to face the public, to becoming a motivational speaker and a coach. Over the years, I have had the privilege of assisting many individuals to overcome their personal and professional challenges. But my journey to becoming a role model for others started with struggles of my own.

The nightmare began when I was forced to resign from my job at the police department as a dispatcher after a crazy night with a rather odd turn of events that led to my wrongful termination. When asked why I was fired, I was given a letter stating I was terminated for "lying and insubordination." I didn't understand it because I had followed protocol. My husband was mayor then but at the time only my boyfriend. He had walked in during the ordeal and handled the situation accordingly, but I was still terminated "for lying and insubordination," which no one had any proof of. And the police Chief recused himself from the investigation. I was forced to go in front of my husband as my boss and leave the hands of this to the board of aldermen. I had to go in front of the City Council with my complaint, and even though it was a "closed session" meeting, there were enough people to cover the entire night shift at the police department. I handed over a printed copy of my complaint and after 30ish minutes of raised voices and heated conversation, I heard the final words, *"We will accept her resignation if we can just get out of here."* I left that meeting feeling numb. Every ounce of self-confidence I had was ripped away that night. I had been betrayed by people who I thought were our best friends. I was changed forever… and then February came…

Three months later, after several incidents of what I would consider borderline hostile encounters at times between my husband and other board members, my husband was handed a letter on Valentine's Day. His "Articles of Impeachment," if you could call them that. It was more like a list of reasons they didn't want him as mayor anymore, but all the same, they were impeaching my husband. On that list, without calling me by name, was my "termination." This would lead to an unimaginable and dark part of my life to depths that I had never seen. And if you knew my childhood, you would understand why. I almost lost both parents to deadly illnesses before the age of 16. But this chapter of my life? This would change my outlook on life completely.

Rumors were flying around, and it was even suggested that the ordeal was my fault. So I found myself in this dark hole, struggling to cope. I was diagnosed with PTSD due to everything that was going on. The news reporter even told me what other city council members said about me the night of the trial: *"She walks around with her nose in the air like she's somebody special"* and, *"She thinks she's Melania Trump!"* That was my favorite; ironically, just a few months earlier, we had dressed up as Donald and Melania Trump for a Halloween Fundraiser Event. But some of the rumors were way worse than that. I had heard everything from I was crazy to I was cheating, and that's not the type of person I am. I loved him too much to cheat, and I wasn't crazy; I was hurt. When it's not just your friends doing this to you, but some of his best ones for over 20 years spearheading it to the point of impeachment, that took a toll on him and me on the whole family, honestly.

During this challenging phase, I joined a network marketing company and connected with a team member who introduced me to mindset shifting. In our first group call, she said, *"Take one negative word a day and turn it into a positive one."* For instance, you wake up, it's Monday morning, and you're running late because you didn't hear your alarm. You ended up leaving the house in two different colored shoes because you tried not to wake your husband and put them on in the dark. You dropped your coffee on the way to the car. Work was horrible because your coworker was in a bad mood, which put you in a worse mood. Everything all day goes wrong, and you get that dread on the way home about not wanting to go in and take that 15-minute break in the car before going inside! (No judgment or shame coming from me, we have all felt this way before)! But you get inside and beat your husband leaving for work; the kids are at the table finishing their homework. And you look at your husband, and he asks, *"What's wrong, Babe?"* but instead of saying, *"I just can't do this anymore…"* you say, *"I'm so blessed to have this life. I CAN do this."* For a couple of months, all worked great with the network marketing, but I soon realized I was helping people but not significantly. I wanted to help with something more centered around making others feel like I did.

This was a turning point as I realized that shifting my mindset was vital in overcoming my struggles. So, I started thinking and talking to my therapist about it and mentioned that I had thought about becoming a Professional Mindset Coach. And she was ALL FOR IT! There is a mental health crisis in the nation right now. Doctors and therapists are flooded and overwhelmed by the number of patients. They are lucky to get more than 10-15 minutes with them, much less help them in ways they can with more extended talk therapy and not just an in-and-out visit.

As someone who always wanted to help people, I was drawn to becoming a therapist when I was younger but going to school was going to take three to four years. A life coach? I could do the course at my own pace. So I began my certification during the appeal process. Eventually, I became a professional life coach with nine niches: self-love, self-care, empowerment, confidence, mindset, spirituality, shamanic, therapeutic art, and goal attainment. I took a few others for my own healing, such as a breathwork facilitator and a crystal healer course. Googling something doesn't usually help much because the truth can come from anywhere, so I wanted accurate, proven methods to heal, and IT DID WONDERS! It was all a distraction from the bad going on around town, and I was gaining my confidence by working on myself; I was back to being better than before, back to a point where telling that story didn't bother me. I was so confident and empowered that I got on *Facebook* Live one night and told my story. When I did… some were upset in town, but at this point, I had done so much work on myself that it didn't matter. I still wore my red bottom high heels to ride backroads. It just rolls right off. I had stopped caring what people thought about how I was "too much." Or too fancy for them or …fill in the blank.

Today, I am proud to say I have helped over 87 women overcome various challenges, including PTSD, anxiety relief through art, grief due to the loss of a parent and a child, and several spiritual breakthroughs. 1:1 coaching sessions for three months is all it took for most. But, just talking to someone and knowing they are giving you things you can do can be a huge confidence booster. Plus you're putting that plan into action for yourself and no one else is telling you that you have to. Of course, you make these choices independently, but you can do simple things to calm or quiet your mind and refocus. I have continued my journey of self-discovery on my own and expanded my expertise by getting certified as a business coach and network marketing strategist. In addition, I'm now a motivational speaker and published author, scaling my business like never before! All thanks to the confidence and empowerment gained from shifting my mindset. There's one thing I keep close by every day. A silly little Post-it note that says **PRONOIA**. Of course, I know what it means, but most don't. Let this sink in as I close out this chapter.

Pronoia- adjective; It's the opposite of Paranoia. Meaning things do not happen to you, and they happen for you. It sounded a little crazy to me at first, but God has a plan for everything. So, if that is the case, then everything happens for me to do the next right thing.

My journey to becoming a coach is the least conventional one ever told. I mean, what First Lady gets her husband impeached for standing up for what was right?? But in all seriousness, my journey to becoming a coach showcases the power of mindset coaching and how I turned a negative experience into a positive outcome by becoming a successful network marketing strategist and a transformational life, mindset, and business coach. And you can too. All you have to do is take the step and ask for help! Sometimes you gotta pull yourself together, slip on a pair of stilettos, put on some bright red lipstick and do what ya gotta do, Sis! It's happening for you, not to you.

Mary Kate Berry is a Transformational Network Marketing Business Coach and Social Media Strategist. Starting out as a Professional Life Coach and Trauma Coach, she is certified in nine niches, including Mindset, Self-Love, Self-Care, Spirituality, Goal Attainment, Therapeutic Art, Shamanic, Cognitive Behavioral Therapy Coach, and REBT Mindset, and finally becoming certified as a Business Coach. She also dabbles in public motivational speaking and has a book in the works about her journey from being a Small Town First Lady to becoming a coach. She has had the privilege of helping many individuals overcome their challenges. But her journey to becoming a role model for others started with her struggles. So, she took a leap of faith, which paid off! Now a successful coach, published author and motivational speaker, she spends her days helping those she relates to best.

Part 5: Setting Your Social on Fire

You know any book I publish is going to include social media. It is the backbone of my business and I have it to thank for the amazing community of Goal Diggers we have built.

When it comes to social media, instead of thinking about the latest trends, I want to challenge you to think about how it fits into your business and what you want it to look like.

For example, do you feel disconnected from your audience because you're holding back? Or do you feel like you're spending way too much time on the app and it's taking over your life?

Whatever it may be, it gets to be whatever you want it to be. It truly is amazing if you know how to create some systems and processes to make it work for you and not the other way around.

Challenge yourself not to settle. Let's make it rock.

CHAPTER 17

Massive Audience Growth through Consistency

by Stephanie Lafler

A little over nine years ago, I ventured into the world of network marketing, a field that was completely new to me. Aside from being what some call a "kitnapper," I had zero experience in this area and had not yet achieved success. At this time in my life my two oldest children were busy playing select sports and both on varsity in high school. We also had a toddler, so to say that we were busy is a bit of an understatement.

I had no idea what I was doing and to be honest, it wasn't even my idea to do this particular business, it was my husband's and I knew my west Texas "cowboy" wasn't going to be slinging wrinkle cream. So, I joined but mostly for the community. My sponsor was someone I adored and wanted to spend time with. Thankfully, she saw in me something I did not and was able to breathe encouragement into me and over my life at a time when I needed it most even though I didn't know it. Despite being my husband's idea, my heart and soul are now forever captivated by this empowering community.

Most of the people in our company were still building belly to belly, so that's what I did. It was at one of those in person events that my sponsor gave me some tough love. She pulled me aside and told me to stop talking about my (super tall and athletically gifted) children and focus on the business. The next words that came out of my mouth will bring tears to my eyes every time I say them out loud to this day . . . *"I don't have anything else to talk about, I'm not interesting."* You might think her words a bit harsh, I did at the time, but you have to understand this was coming from someone who loved me like one of her own children and even though it upset me at the time, I knew she had my best interests at heart. To this day, I appreciate her more than words can express.

At this point in my life, I admit that I had become lost in raising my children. The reason my husband and I had our third child was because I had grown bored with what I was doing. The truth was, I had grown bored of being a fitness instructor and wasn't sure where my path would lead. I had stopped setting goals and forgot how to dream.

There are several things (people/events) over the course of the next few years that made a huge impact on me. One that totally rocked my world was attending a company conference for the first time. Seriously, if you haven't gone to yours yet - what are you waiting for?! The speakers blew me away with their stories of personal development and growth. The author of a book called *The Slight Edge* spoke about making that small decision every day that in the moment might not seem like much but either takes you up the curve of success if repeated over time, or down the curve to failure.

My biggest takeaway from that conference was personal growth. I was an avid reader from the age of eight, reading all 60+ Nancy Drew novels over the course of one summer. My love of reading turned into a bit of an unhealthy addiction to fiction as an adult. I would read or listen to audiobooks pretty much every single day and while reading isn't a bad thing per se, I wasn't doing anything to grow myself or my business by reading murder mysteries or romance novels. I made a commitment to myself on the plane ride home that I would begin with 10 pages a day. Something non-fiction that would help me on my path of personal growth and after 300 books, I stopped counting. In the last eight years since that conference, I've only read one book that was just for pleasure and the funny thing is, I didn't enjoy it as much as I used to. My brain now craves more!

The next event was a conference I attended in October of 2018. It seemed like every time I turned around I heard the word CONSISTENCY. Simon Chan, Purpose Driven Networkers, spoke at that conference and his topic, consistency. Alice Hinckley, who has become a dear friend, also spoke on consistency. It seemed everywhere I turned the message was consistency, consistency, consistency. Getting the memo was easy, but the hard part was putting it into practice. A great book on consistency is *The Consistency Chain*.

I still didn't know much about social media; there was lots of trial and error, mostly error lol. I started with what I had learned from speakers at various training/events and worked on building my consistency muscle.

Every single day, I strive to be better. I am relentlessly pushing myself to achieve consistency in improving my daily method of operation (DMO). I endeavor to go beyond just being busy by creating a productive and powerful routine that encompasses both learning and implementation.

Prior to learning about consistency, I had relied on working when I felt motivated, or basically when I felt like it. Although motivation is a powerful tool for beginning a task, it is temporary and a fickle friend you can't depend on. In contrast, consistency provides a more reliable path to success by helping you remain steady even when motivation leaves you.

When it comes to consistency, it's important to understand that we are all wired differently. If you look at the people in your life, you will see those who are super successful in their business, life, their job, etc. but then, if you look at their personal life or their health/weight, they might look like complete failures. Those people take one approach to their business/profession, and a different approach to other areas in their life. Perfect example… Oprah Winfrey. This was actually me in the reverse! I had figured out how to stay consistent with my workouts, but not yet in my business.

When it comes to consistency, there are very few people that are consistent in every category of their life. The truth is, being consistent isn't easy, but it's worth it.

At this point in my journey, I didn't have social media knowledge or training but longed for a better way to grow and scale my business. There are countless coaches out there dishing out knowledge left and right. But here's the deal: If you try to follow EVERY single one of them, you're going to end up in a state of total and utter confusion. Find one, possibly two that resonate with you and have similar styles, unfollow the rest and get off their email list!

I got introduced to Kimberly Olson through a group where she was doing training on *LinkedIn*. While *LinkedIn* isn't really my jam, this incredible woman really resonated with me and I began to follow everything she did, doing my best to learn and implement what she taught. Meeting her in person at a conference in October 2019 sealed the deal. I adored her and continued following everything she did. I was in her *Goal Digger Mastermind* group where I got to be on Zoom with her and began truly learning about social media.

In January of 2020, I got to be one of her first coaching students when she launched 6FB and that was when I started experiencing true growth. There was also a significant improvement in my productivity and consistency because I knew more of what to do on social media. One of the things I learned from her was how to grow a group. When I got started with her in January, my networking group was at 400 and by the end of the year it was at 1600, now hitting 11K. Kimberly is truly an exceptional coach who has greatly influenced my professional journey.

While our daily activities won't look exactly the same, you have to figure out what the non-negotiables are for you and put them into practice. Track your progress, evaluate it regularly, and adjust as needed.

My daily non-negotiables include:

- Sending birthday messages the day before
- Posting in stories
- Making new connections and scheduling virtual coffees
- Following up with people who watched or interacted with stories
- Posting in my *Facebook* Groups
- Responding to every comment from posts I've made on my personal page and in groups

After I've done that, I choose a few of those people and make sure to interact with their posts as well. As I've heard Fraser Brooks say, you need to give love to get love.

That may sound like quite a bit if you're just getting started but if you're a busy momma like I am, a lot of this can fit into the cracks of your day. If you are like me and love to find shortcuts to help you get more things done in less time, then we should talk a little about automation. If you are open to automation, there are quite a few things that can be taken off your to-do list. Things like sending personalized birthday messages, responding to comments on posts (and sending messages), sending messages to people in your groups and so much more. If this is something you'd love to dive into and need some direction, reach out to me.

Last year my two older children ended up getting married within six weeks of each other and I knew we would be busy! I had to figure out a way to not disappear from social media while we were planning and pulling off those weddings.

Something that I had been doing on a fairly regular basis was short-form videos, reels on *Facebook*, *Instagram* and repurposing for *TikTok*. I began doing that in February of 2022. One reel a day, no matter what. This meant a little planning to make sure I had enough content even on the days I was tired and didn't feel like doing it. I would create multiple videos, typically on Sundays to use for later, incorporating some of our wedding DIY and whatever I felt like doing. I didn't put pressure on myself to be perfect, I just showed up every single day.

You know what the biggest challenge of staying consistent in any activity is? It's learning to release the attachment to the end result. There were days when I started my journey when I would look at the numbers, or lack of interaction and consider giving up. I was busy after all, no one would blame me for a second if I "took a break" but I kept going.

What happened was absolutely amazing! I went from having 1.2K followers on *Facebook* to over 12K, *TikTok* went from 4K to over 9K and I also gained quite a few on *Instagram* as well. All in all, close to 20K across platforms and this seemed to happen almost "overnight." Although, in reality, it transpired due to my consistency and commitment spanning four plus months; the growth happened at a rapid pace once I began to gain momentum.

If you're looking to up your consistency game and need a way to track, I've created a daily calendar where you can check all the boxes that you can download and use for yourself.

Stephanie Lafler is a wife, mother, and Honey (grandma). After 15 years as a fitness professional while raising her first two children, she gave that up for the entrepreneurial life.

Stephanie now helps moms entering the empty nest phase of their life find passion and purpose again while creating a transformative legacy. She's been aligned with a billion dollar anti-aging health and wellness company for about nine years and utilizes their platform to help women create wealth. She's a Christian, social media marketing expert and trainer, personal growth advocate, professional pianist, crafter, and most recently has taken up gardening as a hobby.

CHAPTER 18

Authentically Ausome

by Alyece Smith

When I decided to start showing up on social media for my business, I felt the pressure like a 50-pound weight on my shoulders. How would I make my feed look as aesthetically pleasing as those with teams of people? Or those that had been doing the do for a while and were light years ahead of me? How would I make my pictures look that good with my iPhone? Seriously took a selfies course, ya'll. I started following coaches and leaders in my industry and quickly found myself trying to make my content replicate theirs. This caused so much anxiety in my early entrepreneurial days and ended with many sleepless nights. It caused me to lose sight of why I became an online entrepreneur in the first place - to spend more time with my family. But instead of showcasing my perfectly imperfect life, I spent more time trying to polish and refine it for the *'Gram.* Obviously, I needed to "show up" on social media and put my best foot forward, but I didn't realize that my BEST looked completely different than those I was learning from.

You see, we often are attracted to those we want to be like one day, but we can't compare our chapter two to their chapter 20. Our desire to present a perfect image often compromises our authenticity. We try to fit into the mold that society has set for us, and in doing so, we lose touch with who we really are. And guess what… your audience can TELL! Yes, Girl - they know when you "fake it till you make it."

There is no denying social media has revolutionized the way we interact with each other. We use it to stay connected with friends and family, share our thoughts and experiences, and even build our professional networks; however, we're afraid to be vulnerable and share our imperfections. In doing so, we're missing out on the real benefits of social media - connection.

In this chapter, we'll explore the importance of showing up on social media authentically and how it can benefit us in the long run. Buckle up, Boo; we're rolling on.

Authenticity is *key*. Authenticity is the key to success in a world where everyone is trying to stand out. Sure, trendy *TikTok* dances are cool, but what makes you YOU-nique? When we are authentic, we are being true to ourselves, allowing us to connect with others on a deeper level. People are drawn to authenticity because it's a rare quality to find in this day and age, allowing them to begin trusting you. It's an energy they can feel…even through the screen. Ever posted a piece of vulnerable content, and in your gut thought, can't believe I'm posting this type of content? What happened? More than likely it was way more engaging than others, right?

When we authentically show up on social media, we share a piece of ourselves with the world. We give others a glimpse into our lives, thoughts, and beliefs. This vulnerability can be scary, but it also makes us human. We create a space for genuine connection when we embrace our imperfections and share them with others.

Showing up on social media authentically will always win. It humanizes your personal brand and allows us to build trust with our followers. When we are authentic, we show others that we are real people with real struggles and accomplishments. This makes us real, raw, relevant, and relatable, and people are more likely to engage with us when they feel they can relate.

Authenticity also allows us to attract the right kind of followers. When we are true to ourselves, we attract people who share our values and beliefs. This creates a community of like-minded individuals who support each other and lift each other up. This kind of community is much more valuable than a large following of people who don't truly connect with us.

Showing up on social media authentically isn't always easy, but it's worth it. So how do we do it? Tips for Showing Up Authentically:

1. **Be yourself:** This may seem obvious, but it's worth stating. Don't try to be someone you're not. Embrace your quirks, your flaws, and your unique perspective. Messy bun mom? - cool.. Let's be besties!

2. **Share your story:** Everyone has a story to tell. Share yours with the world. Be vulnerable and open, and you'll be surprised how many people connect with you. Share it repeatedly because you should be growing daily and people need to hear it.

3. **Focus on connection, not validation:** Getting caught up in the likes and comments on social media is easy. Instead, focus on creating meaningful connections with your

followers. Engage with them, respond to their comments, and show them you care.

4. **Take breaks:** Social media can be overwhelming at times. Taking breaks and stepping away from the platform is important when necessary. This will allow you to recharge and return to it with a fresh perspective and creativity.

5. **Know your values:** Understanding your values and beliefs is important. This will help you stay true to yourself and ensure everything you post on social media aligns with your identity.

6. **Be consistent:** Consistency is key in building trust with your audience. Make sure you regularly show up on social media and post content that aligns with your values and beliefs.

7. **Be authentic in your visuals:** Your visuals should also reflect your authenticity. Use images and videos that showcase your real life and personality rather than just using stock photos or overly edited images.

8. **Don't be afraid to share your opinions:** Social media is a platform for expressing your opinions and beliefs. Don't be

afraid to share your opinions on current events or hot topics, but make sure you're respectful of others' opinions as well.

9. **Collaborate with others:** Collaborating with other creators on social media is a great way to build your community and share your message with a wider audience.

10. **Be honest about your intentions:** Don't try to hide your intentions on social media. Be honest about why you're posting what you're posting, and ensure it aligns with your values and beliefs. Showing up on social media authentically is a powerful way to connect with others and build a community. It's also the most successful way to build a business online! It allows us to be true to ourselves and attract the right kind of connections. While it's not always easy, it's worth the effort. By embracing our authenticity, we can create meaningful connections and make a real difference in the world.

Alyece Smith is a mompreneur of three and the owner of *Socially Ausome*. She is a certified Social Media Marketing and Branding Strategist with over five years of experience in Digital Marketing in Corporate America. She is passionate about empowering female entrepreneurs to implement simple social strategies into their businesses to humanize their brand. Currently active in network marketing, affiliate marketing, and as a Social Media Management and Consulting agency owner, Alyece helps others elevate their online presence by making it simple, social, and ausome! She graduated from *Southern Mississippi University* and is a certified Customer Service Xperience Officer.

CHAPTER 19

Automation Domination

by Raenell Edsall-Taylor

Have you ever experienced burnout while running your business? Are there days when you simply do not want to check your phone, respond to messages, make follow-ups with potential clients or prospects, or reach out to existing customers to check in on them? If you can relate to this, know that you are not alone. I have been in your shoes and I understand how it feels.

I like to refer to this as automation procrastination. Why? Because you're putting off the implementation of systems and tools that could automate tasks within your business, thus reducing burnout. Business burnout is a common issue, and failure to develop processes that streamline and optimize your workflow will only exacerbate the problem. Take charge of your time and automate where you can!

Have you ever considered automating your follow-up process with potential clients or prospects, or the onboarding of new team members and customers? Imagine the possibilities – more time to focus on valuable content for social media and building relationships with others. It could even lead to a more manageable and less overwhelming business. How would automation transform your business?

It's time to take control of your automation and go from procrastination to domination. Keep in mind that not everyone has the same tasks that need to be automated. The primary step in freeing up valuable time is to identify the repetitive tasks that are performed on a daily basis that you need to automate so you can focus on your most productive income producing activities.

To establish a strong foundation for your business, let's take it one step at a time and begin by automating your prospecting conversations. As we should know by now, the fortune is in the follow-up. So, wouldn't it be great to have follow-up messages programmed to send automatically every day to prospects? Yes, it's possible, and it only requires some initial setup.

If you haven't already created a follow-up message layout, it's essential to start with one. In my experience with network marketing, I've found it helpful to have follow-up messages prepared for various time intervals. Consider sending a follow-up message 24 hours after discussing pricing and options, followed by another message 48 to 72 hours later.

Then, send messages at one, two, three, and four weeks after the initial discussion. Finally, reach out once a month to maintain contact. Having this follow-up message plan in place ensures that you stay organized and can start the automation process of prospecting automatically.

After finalizing your follow-up message layout, streamline the process by selecting a texting service that can send messages automatically for you. *Project Broadcast* is my personal choice, but there are other options available, too. Most texting services provide tutorial videos to guide you through setting up your campaigns for follow-up messages. The process usually involves either the prospect opting into the texting service or you opting in for them automatically with a keyword. Then allow the automation to take over and send out your prospect follow up messages automatically and give yourself the freedom to focus on the things you truly enjoy.

[If you are interested in seeing how the texting automation works, you can text the word ENCOURAGE to 307-344-1533 to get my 60-days of inspiration through encouragement via text messages.]

This same process can also be used to streamline the onboarding experience for your customers or members too. Simply use a relevant keyword to guide the same process. It's important to plan out your onboarding messages for your customers or members as well. Imagine how much extra time you could have by eliminating this repetitive daily task! Be honest, have you ever found yourself spending hours copy-pasting the same messages to different customers? It can be a tedious and time-consuming process. After I invested time in setting up the automation and conquered procrastination, everything changed. Not only did it save me time, but it also saved my team time too. We all use the same onboarding texting service for all of our customers, so no one has to start from scratch. Simply duplicate what's working and streamline your customer onboarding for your whole team!

Picture this: You receive a text from someone who's interested in the products you love and share. You chat with them to understand their needs and pain points and identify the best products for them. You add them to your automatic follow-up texting system, knowing that it usually takes five follow-ups to close a deal. On the third follow-up message, they decide to make a purchase. After they complete their purchase, you add them to your automatic customer onboarding texting system, where they are guided through the process of using the products they purchased.

However, that's not all – you can also introduce them to the financial opportunities associated with these products through your automatic customer onboarding system by gradually providing small pieces here and there. This way, when they are ready to make a decision to say yes to partnering with you, you can cue them up in your team member's automatic texting system. Are you starting to see the possibilities here?

For my team specifically, when someone partners with me, they get invited to participate in a free 30-day social media challenge. This challenge is designed to teach the ins and outs of social media and how to successfully and effectively promote and share their love of our products with their audience. The 30-day challenge is automated with simple daily steps to help grow their network marketing business.

By utilizing automation, you can effectively free up countless hours in your day. However, it's important to note that this doesn't eliminate human interaction. Instead, it gives you more opportunities to establish genuine connections with individuals. With the time saved from repetitive tasks, you can focus on building relationships with prospects, customers, and team members.

Attempting to automate everything at once can be daunting, and you may find yourself too overwhelmed to make any progress. Instead, break the process down into manageable sections. Start by automating your prospecting process and take time to familiarize yourself with the layout and ideal setup. After that, move onto automating your customer onboarding before finally tackling your team onboarding. Remember, automation is a journey, not a race.

Raenell Taylor is a passionate entrepreneur and a true servant leader who aims to simplify and socialize the selling process through automation and duplication. Her dedication and efforts have earned her a top leadership position in her network marketing company, as well as a feature in *Momentum* magazine. Raenell is a certified

Social Media Marketing Expert and has received direct coaching from the esteemed Kimberly Olson. Beyond her professional accomplishments, Raenell is a gifted speaker who enjoys taking the stage to discuss topics about mindset and building a successful business. Raenell is also a devoted ranch wife and mother of two young cowboys who love to rodeo!

CHAPTER 20

Leading a Winning Team

by Wendy Kat

When I started in Network Marketing, I didn't even know it was an industry. I was a single mom of two kids going through a nasty divorce. A woman from church knew what I was going through and asked how I was doing and for some reason, I decided to be honest with her and said *"I am in my deepest darkest hole,"* and finances were a big part of that. I did not know how I was going to keep the house (because my kids gave me mom guilt and didn't want to move) or even just pay the day-to-day bills. I was working full-time, in a job that paid half my original salary (that's a story for another time) and as a single mom, I didn't have a lot of time. On the sidelines of the football game our sons were playing in, the woman from my church threw me a brochure and said you should do this, come with me and see how I party, and leave with cash in my pockets. I was like, sign me up now.

This was the start of my career in Network Marketing. The first year and a half I just booked party after party, and I was having a blast. Hanging out with amazing women, had some drinks and snacks, and left with money in my pocket. Then my company had a special "join" promotion. Up until this point I did not plug into the company, upline wasn't very involved, and honestly, I was happy just making my money. But with this promotion I had people asking me about "joining." This opened up a whole new world for me; I saw the potential to make some real money and an opportunity to leverage my work effort through *leadership*. I decided to move to a new company that was more aligned with my passions and I went in with a mission to make it to the top rank of the company.

From day one when I signed up, I was already thinking like a leader. That's your first tip; don't wait for a TITLE to make you a leader, you decide you are a leader. You need to step into your leadership and a title isn't what will help you do that. Having a vision is how you set the foundation for creating a successful team. If you are not clear on your goals and how to get there, how can you get your team on board?

Having the right people on your team is key. You want people who are self-motivated, driven, and coachable. You also want people that have a genuine passion for the products or services your business offers. This is why it is so important for you to be clear on your goals so you can show up confidently and energetically which will attract like-minded individuals.

Having an effective recruitment strategy is imperative to growing your team consistently. I find that when leaders don't have a strategy in place they hesitate to invite people into their business. There are two parts of the strategy that are very important. First, have a daily action plan to actively look for new team members, whether it's through social media, networking groups, or referrals. The second part is an "Onboarding" process. If you don't know what you're going to do with your new team member once they join, you are more likely to avoid making the invitation. So please, put a system in place and go out there and recruit with confidence.

Once you have your team members, remember, every type of team member is important to the overall success of your team. The hobbyist, the part-timers, and the rockstars. They all play a role and they are needed. You never know who will bring in your next rockstar, it could be the hobbyist's best friend, you just don't know. Encouraging a collaborative mindset among your team members, and fostering an environment where everyone feels valued, heard, and motivated to contribute their unique skills and perspective is also important.

Once you have a team, you need to train them. I just love helping women build businesses and honestly, this is where things started happening for me. This is when I hit the top rank in my company, "Diamond Director," a whole year earlier than I had planned. I was able to do that because I became a "comp plan" expert. You must know your company's comp plan inside and out. Having this knowledge helps you guide your team to bonuses, promotions, and incentive trips. So many team members get frustrated because of these missed opportunities. This is when you will see team members disengaging and becoming MIA. By staying on top of this you can help close the gap on this happening as frequently. As the leader you have a bigger buy-in and payout in the company and it is in your and in your team's best interest to be on top of this information.

In addition to being a "comp plan" expert, you need to be educating yourself on the industry and continue your self-development journey. I encourage you to read books monthly (*Audible* works, I'm not a huge reader myself!), take courses, join programs, listen to podcasts, etc. These are so important to do so you can pour into your team as you pour into yourself. The cool thing is, you don't have to be an expert in all of these areas right away, you just need to be on the journey. As you learn, you turn around and teach. This is great for many reasons, one it reinforces the training for you, and second you are creating accountability for yourself. Lastly, you inspire others to start their self-development journey.

Creating momentum and keeping it going is the key to long-term success. The best way to do this is to put systems in place to ensure you are motivating your team consistently such as creating monthly challenges, contests, training, etc. It's important that these are built into your team culture so they can count on them and the expectation is there. Recognition may be the most important thing you can do for your team as a leader. For a lot of women, the only place that they will hear a positive statement about themselves or get to be celebrated is with their network marketing company. Often women don't get recognized at home by their spouses, kids, or friends. And a lot of times if they are working a full-time job, they are not getting recognition there either. So be the one that brightens their day and helps them find their light. Being consistent with the way you recognize this will build loyalty to you, your team, and your company.

The best way to lead a team is to lead by example. This means setting a good example for your team members to follow. It also means putting in the hard work and dedication necessary to succeed.

Be patient. Building a successful team takes time. There will be times when your team members are not working their businesses, or not showing up. There will also be times when you feel like giving up. Some of the ways I stay motivated on those hard days are I keep notes from clients and team members thanking me, keeping photos of my kids in sight, and I have quotes and memes that remind me to stay the course. I also have a rule to never decide on the same day that I'm feeling down, I always say *"Let's see how I feel tomorrow."* So far, I have always felt fine the next day! No matter what challenges you face, never give up on your team or your goals. If you are willing to put in the hard work and dedication, you can achieve anything you set your mind to. This is why it is important as a leader to give yourself a long-term goal. Stay focused on the big picture and remind yourself that as an entrepreneur it's normal and expected to have setbacks. Just a reminder that most businesses don't start to see a profit until after five years, so we are way ahead of the game.

Through dedication and consistency in my leadership, my team flourished. The success of my amazing team opened up opportunities for me to speak at several conferences, lead corporate trainings, and earn amazing incentives as a leader. I have developed seven top leaders within my organization. As a team, hundreds of women ranked up many times and earned many incentive trips and bonuses. I didn't even talk about the friendships that are developed and irreplaceable. This network marketing opportunity gave me the opportunity to push myself outside my comfort zone, grow beyond what I could have imagined, and lead me to my dream career. To this day I still get women messaging me about how I impacted their lives and businesses and I don't know about you but that is the best feeling ever!

"If your actions inspire others to dream more, learn more, do more and become more, you are a leader." - John Quincy Adams

Wendy Kat is the Director of Coaching and Enrollment with *GDGC*. As a Master Coach she uses her experience, success-proven strategies, and her no-nonsense approach to coach her students towards success. She is also a single mom of two and has successfully built multiple businesses while working full time and raising her kids. She is the creator of *Leading the Way,* a *Facebook* community where like-minded female entrepreneurs gather for support, motivation, and inspiration. She is also the host of *Leading the Way* podcast. She was a top leader in her network marketing company of eight years and has 30+ years of experience in Sales, Marketing, & Leadership. In addition, she has a B.S in Business/ Marketing and many certifications including "Law of Attraction", "Mindset" and more.

CHAPTER 21

Embrace Your Authentic Power

by Sarah Glenn

Almost overnight, I found myself in the network marketing space, being thrown into 3-way chats and totally confused by all the lingo… upline, sideline, personal volume, AHHH! How on earth does a lifer in corporate America turn into a health and wellness coach just because I bought some products? Clearly, I had no clue what I was doing. Out of pure curiosity, I started to tune into podcasts run by female entrepreneurs, reading books about personal development and quietly observing the people that were finding success around me. I couldn't unsee this new world of possibilities. And so began my entrepreneurial journey.

I never grew up thinking entrepreneurship was an option for me, even though both of my parents were self-employed. Funny how I never heard them call themselves entrepreneurs. Being an entrepreneur implies ownership and complete knowingness that you have the power to create the life you lead. So while they worked paycheck to paycheck, breaking their backs for a buck, that 9-5 life was looking pretty good, pretty safe. But dang it, I was bored!

After many months of feeling confused and unsure of what I was really doing, I knew there had to be a better way. I was not convinced that spamming my newly revived social media profiles was the way to become a millionaire! So I dove into more podcasts, more books and hired my very first business coach. Looking back now, I should have invested in myself sooner. It would have saved me a lot of time, money and energy. But, we live and learn.

So how did I go from confused and frustrated to crystal clear and purposeful? Well, it definitely took intentional effort. But in one word... Belief. Belief in myself, in my ability to do and be different and the willingness to see life from a new perspective. Even if it scared the *ish out of me. Having the mindset of a high-level competitive gymnast for over 15 years, shaped me into a very structured and disciplined person. I was great at punching the clock, but I never saw myself as creative. So the path to becoming a branding expert and mentor was definitely not on my radar.

After a few months of working with my business coach, the belief that I am not creative was smashed! I was seeing proof all around me that I had the innate ability to turn my vision and energy into something beautiful and people started to take notice. I could see that my fellow female entrepreneurs were struggling to be seen, heard and ultimately, confident in presenting themselves as the business owners that they are. The unmet needs of these women led me to create my signature program and ignited a fire in me to show up and become the go-to branding expert that they could turn to.

You now have the incredible opportunity to reveal the essence of you, through your brand. Transcending the "here's my link" mentality and creating meaningful connections with your dream client. Tap into their needs, desires and aspirations. Begin to understand the emotions that drive their decision-making. If you want to make an unforgettable impression and inspire fierce loyalty, spend time getting clear on the essence of your brand. Unapologetically reveal your authenticity and you'll open up a channel for your message to be crystal clear to the right person. It's time to allow yourself to become the undeniable brand that your dream client is magnetized to.

Here's how:

Embrace Your Authentic Power: One of the fundamental pillars of building a successful personal brand is authenticity. Establishing a brand that resonates on an emotional level with your dream client, means you must understand and embrace your own unique identity. You can do this by reflecting on your values, passions, strengths, and desires. Some of the best breakthroughs I've had in my business have come during moments of quiet reflection. So engage in activities like journaling, meditation, affirmations or reading to gain a deeper understanding of who you are at your core. Recognize the patterns and behaviors that feel aligned to you and those that don't. Self-awareness can absolutely become your superpower! By identifying and embracing what you learn about yourself, you can begin to translate your authentic power into a beautifully aligned brand.

TAKE ACTION: Write down your core values. The things that you are passionate about, that light you up and bring you joy. This is how you take the essence of you and turn it into a brand.

Speak To Your Dream Client: These are the individuals who resonate with your message, align with your values, and energetically vibe with what you have to offer. It's time to understand who they are. What their dreams, desires, challenges and aspirations are. Let's not forget about a vital component, actually speaking to them. Aligning your language with theirs and matching their energy helps create a connection that they actually want to engage in. In addition, create content that educates, inspires and entertains. Addressing their pain points and providing solutions. When you are in alignment with your dream client, you inevitably cultivate a community of authenticity and harmony, which leads to deeper connections and long-lasting relationships.

TAKE ACTION: Write down the characteristics of your dream client. What is her name? How old is she? Where does she live? What is her profession? What does she struggle with? What are her hopes and dreams? Be as specific as possible.

Craft Your I Am Statement: This is your opportunity to encapsulate the essence of your brand in a concise and memorable way. This statement is what you want to be known for and should provide clarity on who you are, what you do and what you offer. (Example: I mentor you to create sexy and soulful branding to attract your dream client and scale your business to six & seven figures.)

TAKE ACTION: Draft your I Am statement using this formula; I help/coach/mentor ____, to be/do/have ____ so they can become ____ . Keep it within one to two sentences and play with the words so it sounds like you.

An unforgettable brand goes way beyond a logo or a catchy tagline – it is a promised experience. In an era where everyone wants immediate gratification and the attention spans keep getting shorter and shorter, you need more than a good product or service to stand out. When your dream client feels a genuine connection with your brand, they will become loyal advocates, eagerly sharing their experience and quickly becoming your best brand ambassadors.

By Identifying the essence of your brand, you are giving yourself permission to tap into your true potential, radiate with confidence and attract your dream client. Go ahead and embrace your authentic power and watch how your brand captivates the world.

Sarah Glenn is the founder and CEO of *Social Jane Media;* mentoring you to create sexy and soulful branding that attracts your dream clients and scales your business to six and seven figures. Her mission is to guide you through your journey of self-discovery, creativity and business growth. It's time to let the essence of your brand finally be seen.

CHAPTER 22

Sales Success Secrets

by Rianna Drummond

What often is the first thought that comes to mind when you think of sales? Many times it's the image of a man in a fancy suit pouncing on his first prospects as they walk through a car dealership, the awkward fellow who just won't leave you alone in the electronics department, or the relentless phone calls from some company that you've never heard of!

Sure, these may be some very stereotypical images of sales but what really makes a successful salesperson? What are the real sales success secrets? I can say this, it takes much more than a flashy suit to have real success in sales!

The key to being successful in sales most importantly lies within belief in what you do and the solution you have to offer. If you are passionate about what you are selling and know that it really can be the solution for someone, you have hit the ground running. Without passion and a strong belief that you truly can help someone solve their problem or meet their wants, you are like a ship lost in a turbulent sea. If you experience what you are offering and really believe in it...if you have felt the benefit or experience some elation of emotion when you talk about or engage in it, selling will be easy and people will want what you have to offer. If the passion isn't there it is like rubbing stone upon stone and your audience will feel the friction! If the belief, passion, and excitement in what you are 'selling' is there, what you have to offer won't even feel like selling. You won't have to struggle and coerce. You won't have to feel the need to convince. It won't be a burden or stress.

People will come to you because they want to experience that same passion you feel for what you have. Your audience will believe you because you are practicing what you preach. They are inclined to come to you because they see the benefit you are getting from what you are doing and believe that you know exactly what you are talking about. You aren't making things up and pretending to know it all. You actually have learned, participated in, and experienced what you are selling. Your audience will see you as the expert and have a built-in trust in what you do because you have proven to them by your actions and example that you have the solution for them.

To build on this, actions alone aren't simply enough. To be successful, consistency is key! Being consistent in what is done and in your actions is the foundation in building audience trust. After all, would it make sense to buy from someone who is all over the place and doesn't seem to have all the pieces of the puzzle in order?

People are drawn to positivity and when you believe in something and really know it works, you are more positive and that attracts. If the dark cloud of negativity looms overhead and you just don't really believe in what you are offering, how can you expect your audience to want what you have?

People won't have the trust and feel forced. Forcing a prospect into a sale is a failed sale. Ultimately, people like to feel in power and have a sense of control over the decisions they make. To have a successful sale, you will want the prospect to be confident with their decision and to really buy what you offer because they fully feel it is the solution for them. If they are pushed into a sale, there is a resistance that won't go away and they are unlikely to be satisfied or get any results from what you have provided them.

There has to be a want and need for what you are offering. What is more important is that they can't just have one or the other. You may believe they need what you are offering but if they don't want it, there will be that resistance and ultimately, dissatisfaction.

A successful sale comes from the customer experience and journey with you. In order for you to have a journey with a customer it is critical to first identify and understand 'who' your ideal avatar really is. This involves a deep analysis into what your avatar wants, the struggles and challenges they face, and the dreams they have. It's easy to target everyone and believe you will create success in numbers but the success really stems in who you are actually doing business with. You also need to honestly feel that the prospect will benefit from what you have to offer or find a solution from it. Your customer then needs to understand the value in what you have to offer and that the benefit they will get from it exceeds the price.

More importantly, they need to be able to afford what you have to offer. If your customer is put in a financially detrimental position or setback by purchasing from you, you are not being a solution. We want to remember 'successful sales are solutions.' Creating setbacks and putting the customer in an uncomfortable position would be a problem and contrary to the goal of a successful sale. Your customer may be able to afford what you have, want and need what you have, and you may give them the results they are looking for but it is very important to understand your job is not finished.

The customer experience extends past the purchase. What does this mean? Any successful salesperson will continue to build their relationship with their customer. They will be there to serve them after the dotted line has been signed. They will answer questions, offer help, and go above and beyond to ensure customer satisfaction. The measures they take to create customer satisfaction and results for their buyer will lead to referrals. By being diligent in creating a hospitable and serving environment, you are able to increase buyer loyalty and trust. A customer who is served after the purchase is made will be highly likely to repurchase from you and recommend your services or products to others. By providing that service, you will reap the benefits of word-of-mouth sales.

If we are able to sell something we believe in, have a passion for it, and understand completely what we are doing… we can have a successful sale. If we identify our ideal avatar and work with them to feel a sense of control in their decision making and serve them to the best of our ability…we can have a successful sale. If we show our customer that we have the solution to their problem and fulfill their wants...we can have a successful sale. If the customer really is able to see value over price and reasonably work with us...we can have a successful sale. If we are able to serve our customer after the sale and show true care and consistency in our actions, we genuinely can say we have provided the ultimate customer experience and have unlocked the secret of sales success!

Rianna Drummond is from Alberta, Canada. She lives with her husband, two kitties, and her new baby girl. She is a Goal Digger Concierge and has been working on the team since Jan 2023. Rianna comes from a background in sales in the fitness industry which she had been doing 17 years prior. She also achieved her Life Coaching Certification last year. Rianna loves helping people better their lives both mentally and physically and was very drawn to *Goal Digger Girl Co*

to work as she saw the huge opportunity in helping people become successful with their businesses!

Part 6:

Conquering

Productivity

The theme of conquering productivity has been coming up a lot from clients I work with and as a requested topic when I do any kind of guest training or speaking. So if you feel stressed out just thinking about reigning in your to-do list, we've got you.

The truth is, we all have the same 168 hours in the week. It's how you use your time, set up your schedule and say yes or no to things that makes all the difference.

Entrepreneurs by nature are very creative and we tend to squirrel a LOT. I understand. I always got in trouble for talking in school and got approved to finish school off campus in college when that wasn't a thing yet. Sitting still? No thank you, lol.

Learning how to master your time is going to change your life. You will go from never feeling successful when it comes to your daily productivity to feeling like a freaking rockstar.

CHAPTER 23

Setting Yourself Up for Success

by Courtney Koenig

On January 3, 2022, I woke up feeling completely normal. I did my usual morning routine of listening to a spiritual message, journaling, and cleaning up the house. Then, I started working on client deliverables and drinking my smoothie. Halfway through my smoothie, I started to feel sick. The chills came on and I felt so weak. I grabbed a bunch of blankets and climbed back into bed. I canceled my work meetings. I felt so sick so quickly. Seven days later I was still sick, but I had different symptoms. I tested positive for Covid that day. The same day I started having neurological symptoms of slow mental response time, uncoordinated movements, neuropathy mixed with Covid symptoms. I went to the ER because I was having very unusual, scary symptoms. The ER did a CT scan and said I needed to see a neurologist. I did not think that was a very helpful visit. I wanted answers! I wanted to feel better!

I found a neurologist and she scheduled several MRIs and a spinal tap. After all the tests, my husband and I met with the doctor. She walked into the room and just got right to the point. She said I had MS. I am the kind of person who, when I find out answers, I immediately want to know the next steps or solutions. I asked her what I should do next and when I would feel better. The doctor responded and said she needed to find a medicine that would work for me which might take some time. I was okay with that. *"Once we find that medicine,"* I asked, *"when will I be back to normal?"* She responded that we would try to get me to feel as good as possible but she had no idea what that would look like. I was so shocked by that answer! I was thinking that was a pretty crappy answer.

That crappy answer changed everything for me. After a couple of days of letting the doctor's answer settle in, I realized that if I wanted to feel better, I had to take caring for myself very seriously. I remember telling my friends about the diagnosis and telling them what I have control over is taking care of myself. Even though I took care of myself before, I knew this diagnosis meant that my body needed a new level of care and support.

I had always pushed myself in business and in life. I would go to the gym and do cardio super intensely. I would push myself in my business to expand into more countries, with more clients, and with more programs. It is not that what I did was too much, it was that I never acknowledged all that my body, my mind, and my heart was doing. I didn't celebrate my accomplishments. I was not celebrating who I was becoming. I moved through my checklist and jumped onto the next launch, offer, or meeting.

The meaning I had assigned to my life and business was through the lens of overachieving, perfectionism, and unrealistic expectations. I realized how hard I was on myself. I really wanted to have more peace in my life and in my business. I realized that I could only have as much peace as I was willing to drop overachieving, perfectionism, and unrealistic expectations.

I figured out two questions to ask myself that helped me embrace peace and ignite lots of joy in my life and business:

What is my part and what is not my part?

How can I celebrate today?

What is my part and what is not my part?

I love Taylor Swift! My daughters and I went to her concert and it was so amazing. One thing Taylor does so well is that she performed and connected with the audience. The concert we went to was sold out with around 60,000 people. When

Taylor appeared on the stage, the whole building shook with excitement. She sang, danced, ran up and down the stage, and changed outfits multiple times. She did this for three hours. She did her part which is to use her talent to entertain the audience. She also connected with us. It was so beautiful to feel her positive energy. Taylor's part was to sing. Her part was not to get everyone to buy more merch, set up the beautiful moss-covered piano, or control the lighting. She showed up and did her thing with love, enthusiasm, and passion.

Often, we try to do everyone's part. We don't need to. We can release what is not ours and embrace our part. We can show up just like Taylor with love, enthusiasm, and passion for ourselves and others.

How can I celebrate today?

We have a dog named Holland. He is a cute little black poodle. He has an attitude but he is so cute so he can totally get away with it! When we first got him, I really wanted to take him on walks. I knew it would be so important to my health. At the beginning of my healing journey, it was hard for me to walk to the mailbox. I really wanted to take Holland on a very short walk around the block. I started with a very short walk to the end of my cul-de-sac. Then from there, I extended it a little bit longer. After each walk, no matter how long it was, I celebrated. I was so proud of my body for being able to move. It felt so good to take a moment to honor what I was doing.

I celebrate a lot in my life and business! I celebrate each time I receive a new client, each time Stripe sends me a payment, each time I record a podcast, each time I expand to a new country, each day when I listen to my body and take a nap, each time I go to the gym and lift weights, and more.

My life and business have been forever changed. It has a layer of peace and happiness that doesn't come from accomplishing to-dos but through doing my part and celebrating.

Courtney Koenig is an International Human Design and Manifestation coach. She ignites business owners to become more powerful, profitable, and purposeful. She is a certified business Master Coach and Human Design Reader. She lives in Dallas with her husband of 27 years and four kids, two dogs, and one grand dog. She loves *Netflix*, naps, and sparkling water.

CHAPTER 24

Getting Tech to Work for YOU

by Steph Dakin

Do you have a love/hate relationship with technology? Working behind the scenes at *Goal Digger Girl Co,* we find that many entrepreneurs have trouble leaning in to all that technology can do for them. And while tech *can* be challenging, it can also be your most efficient, hardest working employee that frees you and your actual team members up to do more of what you do best. Not only can you have it work for your business, you can also use it to manage your home and your family.

Here's what I mean.

If you have birthdays or other repeating events that you want to keep track of, using an online calendar (like *Google Calendar*) allows you to set that event to *automatically* repeat for you every year. You can set custom reminders to notify you well in advance of the event in case you need to order a gift or get a card in the mail.

You can set daily or weekly reminders for those work tasks that you don't want to forget - just make sure that you open and assess your calendar each day. Using this method, you can use your calendar as a to-do list. Using the functionality of your particular calendar, there are different ways you can "check off" the task as you go, such as changing the color of the event or editing the name of it. Many email providers will even let you turn an email into a task on your calendar as an additional reminder to check on that task in the future.

When it comes to keeping your email organized, create folders (sometimes called "labels" by certain email providers) and file away any emails that you no longer need sitting in your inbox, but that you're not ready to archive or delete. Keeping your inbox pared down will ultimately keep what's most important in front of you and anything else that has been handled is easy to search for if you ever need to reference it again.

For those of you who tend to be forgetful or get so engrossed in what you're doing that you lose track of time, setting timers for yourself can be a lifesaver. I check my calendar first thing in the morning and review any time-sensitive activities - meetings, places I need to be, etc. I'll set a timer for a few minutes before that meeting, or just before I need to leave the house if it's a doctor's appointment, etc. If you have an *Amazon Echo* (aka 'Alexa') or *Google Home* device, you can verbally tell it to set those timers for you. You can set the timers on your phone if that's more convenient, but whatever you use, I recommend something that you can set all of your timers for the day at one time rather than having to set a new timer every time it goes off.

If you're collaborating online like our team does (we're scattered all over the US, and even Canada), using *Google Sheets & Google Docs* is huge, as is *Trello* (you can get a free account at Trello.com). These apps make it easy to share templates and read-only versions with others which is great if you are duplicating your efforts with a team and want everyone using the same prospecting tracker, social media planner, etc.

We also use *Trello* for a Customer Relationship Manager (CRM) and to keep track of repetitive tasks that we need to do when we are launching something new. Having some kind of tool that will let you copy checklists over and over again can be incredibly valuable whether you're planning an online event, like a Masterclass Series, or an in-person event, like a party. You could even use these repeating checklists for your staple grocery items that you tend to buy over and over. This frees your brain up by not having to remember the small details each time and keeps you from missing or overlooking any details.

Our family uses an app called *Cozi* where we have a shared grocery checklist. *Cozi* allows you to set up a family password so that all family members can access the list from their phones and add to it as we think of things that we need. The person doing the grocery shopping (usually my amazing husband!) can check off those items as they're purchased, and anything that we couldn't find from the list can be carried over for next time. *Cozi* has the convenient functionality of letting you delete all checked items from the list if you choose to, so you can uncheck anything that you want to keep for next time and delete the rest. There are also calendar sharing options in the app, though we haven't explored those yet.

If you have a team and you find yourself teaching the same thing to each and every person, you would benefit by creating a training video library and directing each new team member to that training library. A simple version of this can be created within a private *Facebook* group. You can go live directly in the group, or you can use *Zoom* if you need to share your screen on video. If you use *Zoom*, the recordings can be downloaded and uploaded to the private *Facebook* group. This maximizes your time as a leader, and everyone gets the same training regardless of when they join your team.

One of my favorite ways to use technology in business is to automate repetitive tasks, particularly when they have multiple steps to them. Many of the larger online platforms will integrate with others, so you can use a calendar app like *Calendly* for letting people book online appointments with you, and it will automatically integrate with your *Zoom* to send them the link to join you at the appointed time, as well as with your calendar. Other platforms will integrate your sales pages with your email list, so when you have a new sale your prewritten welcome message goes out to your new client letting them know important next-steps.

We like to take our integrations a few steps farther, using a platform called *Zapier*. Using this app, we can automatically enroll our clients into the appropriate course, add them to a worksheet where we keep track of clients, add them to the CRM *Trello* board that I mentioned earlier, and more. This, once again, frees up brain-power as the automation will handle these repeat tasks for you on the back-end.

While technology is not infallible, I am a firm believer that it is an incredibly valuable tool for entrepreneurs and household managers alike. If you want to be able to grow and scale your business, the possibilities are endless with the creation of new apps and platforms. While tech is constantly changing and evolving, by figuring out what components you need the most right now, you can find the right tools for your budget and grow from there.

Steph Dakin is the Client Experience Director at *Goal Digger Girl Co.* She is a Christian, a wife, a mom of two teens, and a self-proclaimed tech nerd who loves the satisfaction of solving a good tech mystery. She is passionate about helping entrepreneurs who view technology as a stumbling block to their business get unstuck. Growing up, Steph watched her family own and run several businesses, and so she's always had an entrepreneurial spirit.

CHAPTER 25

Slow & Steady Wins the Business Growth Game

by Pamela Hilton

Most people start their business with accounting as an afterthought..."*Oh yeah, I guess I need to keep track of these numbers so I can file my tax returns this year.*" I want to change that. I want to change the way people think about accounting.

My name is Pamela Hilton. I am a Certified Public Accountant licensed in Massachusetts. I have over three decades of experience working with individuals and businesses, saving them money and helping to increase their growth and profits.

Like most, I love to scroll social media and read people's stories. There is no shortage of girl bosses who seemed to have shot to fame and now earn a seven-figure income overnight. This is not my story. As an only parent, I had to simmer my business on a back burner for years waiting patiently to shoot my shot.

Back in the early 90's, my journey into business ownership started like most CPAs. Not long after I graduated from

Bentley College, family and friends would ask if I could do their taxes. This is typical for most CPA's - to start as a tax preparer using *Staples* bought software, but where I took a bit of a different path eventually proved to be the key to my success even if I didn't know it at the time.

When I graduated, all the big, national accounting firms were heavily recruiting at my college. Everyone with an accounting major wanted to work for one of these major firms. This did not interest me at all. If you were hired by a large firm you were either put in their tax department where you worked ridiculously long hours during tax season, or you were in their audit department working similar hours and traveling constantly. Neither of these appealed to me, I wanted the job experience that included tax AND audit, I wanted to do it all. And so, I did- I chose to work for a smaller CPA firm that gave me hands on tax, audit and accounting experience I never would have gotten at a large national firm. This path allowed me to experience all phases of the business process: sales, customer relations, inventory management, marketing, bill payment, cash flow cycles, and so much more from start to finish across dozens of industries. Auditing, tax preparation, payroll, bookkeeping, tax planning, all of this created a unique education that is now the framework for my firm today.

Now, 30 years later, I have a boutique firm that offers clients a customized, tailored accounting and tax package of services with flat-fee pricing. Now I know that flat fee subscription pricing is the norm now, but 20 years ago when I was creating my business model this was not as popular and CPAs were not doing this. In fact, other CPAs I worked with thought I was crazy and I'd never have a profitable business this way. I knew that's what clients needed – dependable services with a consistent monthly fee. Why should any service be open ended? Why can't clients know in advance how much their accounting and tax prep fees were going to cost them for the year?

Well, it turns out, that's exactly what they wanted and needed. I have built my very successful practice with this model of monthly accounting services with annual tax planning and tax preparation for businesses. The response from our clients has been overwhelmingly positive and my firm continues to thrive and grow with this model.

How did I originally grow my practice? When I first started, I acquired almost all of my clients the old fashion way, direct mail. That's right, a carefully written marketing letter sent to a mailing list of newly incorporated businesses. Good old snail mail style. Employing this method accelerated my practice to six figures with clients that are still with me 25 years later.

I began this marketing campaign as a single parent of two. I worked part-time per diem at another CPA firm, ran my small firm on the side and sent out letters by the hundreds each year. I was a single mother, running my own business and the primary caretaker and only earner for me and my young daughters. I was grateful that my kids loved grilled cheese and apple slices because that's what they got most days, things were sometimes tight financially. I was only able to grow my firm to a certain level so I'd be able to still provide my clients with a high level of services yet still be able to raise my kids – drive them to and from school and sports, stay home with them when they were sick, do all those things a parent needs to do all while trying to run a business and work part-time. Due to the demands of being an only parent, with little to no help, I had to keep my firm small and manageable. When they say you can have it all, it's true- to a point. Sacrifices need to be made to have it all and for me it was my social life and the growth of my business. I grew it just enough to be financially stable so I could be a present parent. It was important to me to be a mother first and business owner second, my clients knew this and so did my children.

My plan all along was that once my daughters were grown, I would have the time and freedom to see how big I could grow my firm. As they got older, began to drive and got their first jobs, I started to shift my business focus. Instead of just keeping my firm small and manageable, it was time to grow and hire staff. That was only a few short years ago back in 2019. In 2020, I started to look into social media as a marketing tool to replace my tried and true (and outdated) direct mail system.

I am an introverted extrovert (emphasis on the introvert part) and I had zero social media presence. I had a very standard website that I made no effort to market or even cared if it showed up in online searches. No *Facebook*, no *Instagram*, and an incredibly sad *LinkedIn* account. If you know anything about finance people – they are notoriously terrible at marketing.

I waded into the social media pool first with *Facebook* and then with *Instagram*. What I found was that people were desperate for business and accounting knowledge and advice. There is very little support and opportunity out there for businesses to learn about taxes, finances, and accounting. Using the tools from business coaches, I set into action some very consistent principles to my online presence – add value, be authentic and don't be salesy.

In less than three years using social media I have grown a solid following on *Instagram* and consistently have prospects reaching out to me each week. It has not been a rocket to fame and fortune like some others on social media, but this slow and steady growth is working for my firm, increasing revenue and our online reputation. You could say that I am the tortoise not the hare with respect to social media growth. As a business owner of 30 years, I have learned that it is not how fast you grow, but that your growth is consistent and sustainable.

I have learned a lot over my long and successful career and if I could share some advice to help others it would be this:

- Don't compare yourself to other businesses or people. You are a unique entity and need to create your own path and business model that works for you.

- Find your tribe. I did it alone for too many years until I just recently found my tribe, both online and with an in-person women's business group. It has been a game-changer for me. Yes, you are smart but it never hurts to have other smart women around to boost you up and bounce ideas off of.

- Seek out solid professionals to mentor and build your business foundation– you need these five: A CPA, lawyer, insurance agent, bank/lender, and financial planner.

- Never underestimate accounting – it's the language all businesses have spoken for centuries and it's one of the most powerful tools your business has. It's not just a record keeping system so you can do your taxes; when done properly accounting is the foundation that your entire business is built upon and the road map for its growth and success. If you are not a numbers person, then educate yourself on why accounting is crucial and strive to make enough to outsource this part to a solid and trustworthy professional.

- Don't get discouraged if it takes a little longer for you to find success. Look at me, it took decades, but I wouldn't have it any other way.

I hope that my story can inspire other single parents and business owners. It's a lot of hard work, but you can do both. And I also hope that I can change the way you feel about accounting; it's important to get the numbers right for your business to succeed.

Pamela Hilton is a Certified Public Accountant and the owner of *Pamela L. Hilton, CPA Inc.* Pamela started her career over 30 years ago in public accounting where she learned a hands-on and personal approach to tax and audit services. This experience is the basis she used to build her successful practice that offers clients a deep knowledge of business processes, taxes and accounting systems. You can find her on *Instagram* and *Facebook* (@pamelahiltoncpa), offering free business, accounting and tax advice to her audience. Pamela is an only parent to two daughters and currently resides in Haverhill, MA.

CHAPTER 26

Organizational Tools for Peak Productivity

by Abby Ascencio

It was my senior year of High School when I was voted class neatest and class most organized. At first, it may have seemed like a small achievement, but as I carried on in my life, I realized the immense importance of effective organization. By taking time to set up organizational systems, we can simplify our lives and streamline our tasks, allowing us to focus on what truly matters. Through my own experiences, I've seen firsthand the benefits of having a clear plan and system in place. Organization is a key ingredient in achieving success and achieving it with ease.

As a self-proclaimed organization guru, I've tested out a plethora of platforms and methods designed to keep us all sane and on-task. From *Asana* to *Monday*, *Evernote* to *Todoist*, I've navigated my fair share of productivity tools. But it's not just the modern software that I've explored - I've gotten my hands on the *Pomodoro* technique, *Kanban* boards, and even the 80/20 rule. While some of these methods proved to be game-changers for me and my work, others left me feeling flustered and stressed. However, my experimentations have left me with valuable insights into the most effective ways to stay organized in a professional setting.

As an entrepreneur, I wear many different hats throughout the day so my schedule is jam-packed with a variety of tasks that require my utmost attention. Did I mention I have a daughter who recently turned 13 and an 8-year-old son that never seems to get tired? I would pay millions to have his energy! If you can relate to this fast-paced lifestyle, don't worry, because I have a solution that will revolutionize the way you go about your day. Get ready to say goodbye to disorganization and hello to efficiency for streamlining your workload.

Trello - Trello provides a simple yet powerful visual tool to efficiently manage any type of project, workflow, or task tracking. You can customize the platform to adapt to your unique work style. So whether you're working on a large product launch or creating a meal plan for your family, Trello offers the tools you need to maximize your productivity! Here are some of the boards I've created for both my business life and mom life:

Content Bank - As a content creator, it requires coming up with new ideas, staying in touch with trends, and ensuring your audience remains engaged and connected. To remain relevant and interesting, I use a content bank to save all the potentially useful things I come across, from graphics to quotes to other ideas that come up while I'm washing the dishes. With my content bank at the ready, I never have to worry about struggling to find new ideas for social media posts. The wealth of inspiration I have at my disposal ensures that I can plan out a month's worth of content without ever feeling like I'm creatively drained.

Repurposing Bank - With the ever-growing demand for fresh content on multiple social media platforms, it can be overwhelming to come up with ideas on a daily basis. Thanks to the concept of repurposing content, we can save time and energy while still maintaining a consistent presence online. By creating a Repurposing Bank, content creators can easily access pre-approved posts that have already proven to be successful. By saving every piece of content that can be repurposed, you can build a bank of reusable content to choose from when you need to post.

Engagement Bank - In today's social media world, engagement is key. There is nothing quite like waking up to a flood of comments on your latest post. That's why I've spent the last four years adding engaging and attention-grabbing questions to my bank of go-to posts. Whenever I see an engagement question that is generating a lot of buzz and traffic, I quickly add it to my bank. This way, I always have fresh content to post and can promise my clients a high level of engagement. Within my Engagement Bank, I have carefully crafted categories of questions. Some of the questions are about network marketing, branding, goal setting, self-care, entrepreneurship, *Instagram*, and even mom life. With my Engagement Bank at the ready, I can attract endless comments and ensure my content is always engaging.

One of my favorite reasons for sticking with *Trello* is because I was finally able to find a good system for my tasks. After trying out numerous methods, I was at a loss for how to efficiently manage my daily tasks, especially with my type of fast-paced work. On an easy day, I have new tasks, special projects, and last-minute requests being sent to me and every task is equally important so it was my job to assure every task was completed and I met every deadline. I've been determined to try out different types of to-do lists; I even looked into experts' methods and tested them out. Unfortunately, none of these were suited for me. Post-its stuck on the desk seemed like a good idea until one of my cats walked away with one. *Trello* offers a customizable system that allows for easy organization, prioritization, and tracking of tasks. Unlike other methods, where I would only use for about a month, I've been using *Trello* for over seven months now and am still satisfied with its effectiveness.

Many people often assume that *Trello* is only for streamlining their business activities. However, the truth is, *Trello* is a versatile tool that can be used to make life easier in so many ways, especially for busy moms. That's where my Weekly Meal Plan board, Budgeting board, Gifts board, and Kids School & Activities boards come into play. These boards have truly transformed the way I can manage and plan my family's life. I can say goodbye to the stress of meal planning, as I have all my recipes organized in one place. The Budgeting board helps me keep track of my expenses and savings, while the Gifts board ensures I'm always prepared for Christmas gift ideas, birthday gift ideas, anniversary gifts, and any other special occasion. And on my Kids School & Activities board, I can keep track of everything from school assignments to extracurricular activities and fun at-home projects. I've been able to plan my children's birthday parties and our family road trips. *Trello* has helped me keep track of all the details and ensure that everything runs smoothly. More recently, my daughter and I even used *Trello* to start working on our family tree.

I have found *Trello's* features to be a game-changer for project management! As someone who relies on efficient procedures, I've created a board specifically dedicated to all types of procedures. This could include anything from the steps needed to execute a successful masterclass to the tasks necessary for an in-person mastermind event. The real magic, however, lies in its detailed checklists. Every task, no matter how small, can be listed and checked off, ensuring that nothing falls through the cracks. These procedures act as a blueprint to guide you through the necessary steps to complete a successful project. You will not only increase your efficiency during your current project, but you will also set yourself up for success for future projects. Establishing a process for each step of the project allows for a streamlined approach and alleviates the stress of having to figure out what to do next.

David Allen's quote, *"Your mind is for having ideas, not holding them,"* has had a huge impact on the way I work. A seemingly simple line captures just how valuable our minds truly are. We all do our best to fill our mental hard drives with everything from meetings to packages that need mailing but the truth is this frantic juggling act of tasks only exhausts our brains instead of fostering creativity. The solution? Taking advantage of external tools such as *Trello*. David Allen imparted more than brilliant wisdom- his thinking reminds us we control the power of reflection if only we remember what energizes and what exhausts our greatest asset: our minds.

Being organized is the key to success in any professional field. The ability to efficiently manage our time and workload is paramount to achieving great results and elevating our work to the next level. Personally, being organized not only allows me to work faster and more efficiently, but it also affords me more time to develop new skills and explore ways to create better ideas. More importantly, I'm able to channel my focus towards professional growth without being bogged down by the overwhelming details that often come with the job. As a result, staying organized has not only facilitated my work, but has also contributed a great deal to my overall professional development.

Being an entrepreneur surely has its perks but long hours, late nights and even working from Monday to Sunday was the norm for me. It meant that this often meant missing out on quality time with my family, which led to immense mom guilt. I had a tough time prioritizing and organizing all the tasks I had in front of me; staying focused and completing them just wasn't happening. Even though I was sitting at my desk surrounded by all sorts of to-dos, multitasking was such an automatic reflex for me that jumping from one task to the next without finishing anything didn't feel odd. When it comes to professional growth – being organized turned out to be a powerful benefit, but the biggest reward that came along with it has been the extra time I now get to spend with family.

Abby Ascencio is an accomplished entrepreneur hailing from the windy city of Chicago, IL. Abby's journey through the world of business management, sales, marketing, and social media management has taken her to where she stands today. Abby began as an office manager for six years where she was responsible for overseeing an efficient team of secretaries and quickly transitioned to being the Executive Assistant for the CEO of the company for over four years. Not one to shy away from exploring new opportunities, Abby ventured into the world of children's entertainment, launching a successful face painting and art business bringing joy to countless children's faces for five years! Seeking a position that would allow her to spend more time with her kids, Abby transitioned into network marketing. This led her to collaborate with her sister-in-law on a new venture – a social media management business explicitly catering to Top Leaders in the Network Marketing industry. She strongly believes that her entire business journey was preparing her for when she landed her dream job with such a prestigious company, *Goal Digger Girl Co*, as the Creative Director.

CHAPTER 27

Wearing the Hat YOU Want to Wear

by Andrya Martin

"We are afraid to allow ourselves to blossom fully because of the general disapproval that fills our air whenever a 'little lady' forgets her place." -Marianne Williamson

Have you ever forgotten your place or who you are called to be? I know I have many times. The pressures we face as women to be all to everyone, and everything, to fit into a certain mold is mind boggling. Is this really the way it's meant to be? Is there a better way?

We all love a good hat; it hides our imperfections in so many ways. Just maybe, we need to take off the hats. We hear it all the time, women wear so many hats and it's true. There are so many, but during this time let's look at three. The baseball cap, the toboggan and the hard hat.

The baseball cap is hanging by the door, as she leaves the house on her head it goes, her hair is thrown in a ponytail, she is ready to conquer the day. She is juggling so many things. Dropping the kids off at school, maintaining the home, career, friends, family, school activities, play dates, oh, I almost forgot a healthy meal that needs to be on the table by six o'clock.

What about the lady in the toboggan? It's a different season in her home now. She keeps everyone warm, inside on those bad days, she tries to maintain an atmosphere of peace and coziness within her home life, family relationships and friendships. She is a peacekeeper. She is not a stir the pot type of gal. She lets a lot of the things slide. She knows she will step in and pick up the pieces when things get messy. Her gentleness is an open door for hurt, abuse and pain.

Lastly, we have the hard hat woman, she has it covered, and nothing is getting through her shield of protection. She is the CEO of her own company, possibly a wife, mother, caregiver, PTO President, organizer of a non-profit, homeschool momma, excellent negotiator, chauffeur, protector, provider, counselor, gatekeeper, vision holder and all-around woman on the move. She does it all and appears to have it all together.

But does she?

Many times, we say yes when we are asked to help or serve knowing our heart is not into it. We jump to the rescue of others because seeing someone suffer is not on our radar, especially if we can fix it. See, many of us are fixers. Who else can raise their hand and say, that's me? We will take on the task knowing there is a price we will pay mentally, emotionally, physically, or even spiritually. But we are willing. We wear all of these hats without ever asking is this MY BEST YES?

I see this on a daily basis in my practice. As a Functional Nutrition Counselor and Holistic Health Coach, I see women wearing so many hats. Many have let these hats consume their lives, neglecting their own self-care and who they are called to be. Society has told them their role. They have not taken the time to be still and ask, *"Who am I, what is my purpose?"*

They end up exhausted, burned out, overwhelmed, addicted, broken, depressed, hurt, neglected, withdrawn, disease ridden and on the brink of a full body meltdown. You might ask, how do I know? Because I was that woman. I was wearing all the hats and many more. Your hats will change as you go through the different seasons. I learned many lessons along the way, and I hope you can glean from my experience.

I want to share some of those lessons with you. Today I'm celebrating my 56th birthday. I would never have thought that today on my 56th birthday, I would become an author. It was on my bucket list. Thank you, Kimberly, for giving me my first opportunity. You are a blessing and I love you! Sorry I digressed, but this woman is a jewel! Stay tuned, I have another book already in the process. Hold on, did I say 56? My youngest son keeps reminding me that I'm so close to 60! I have to laugh; I feel like I'm just getting started! Life is what you put into it, one moment at a time. At one point, I thought 60 was old but now I know age is just a number. That number doesn't need to define you in health, physical ability, mental stability, emotional guidance or your purpose.

Things I've learned along the way:
- Self-care needs to take a higher place of priority.
- A bad moment, hour, day, week, month or year does not make for a bad life.
- Life is tough, you can overcome it.

- Let the little things go, don't make mountains out of molehills.
- You will fail, your kids will fail, your spouse, partner, business partner will fail, failure is part of life, learn from it and move on.
- Don't hold grudges, forgive and let go. Maybe, you need to forgive yourself, do it, you are not called to be captive to your failures.
- Unconditional love goes a long way, and you need it for yourself too.
- Never settle, life is too short and there is a plan for you greater than you can ever imagine, you are made for more.
- It's okay to say NO and set boundaries.
- Words have power, they can bring life or death, choose life.
- Setting a daily time to be still, listen and reflect is so valuable and important for spiritual health. Movement is key, it helps with our physical and mental state.
- Nature is to enjoy and to experience the beauty of creation.
- It's good to have fun, laughter is great medicine.

- True friendships matter and will lift you up when you are down.
- Real friends want to see you win!
- Last, but not least, I matter, I have needs. I need to see and honor the value within myself as a woman who needs care, love and attention.

Have I arrived? No. Do I always get it right? A big no. And we all are a work in progress. Remember, this is a journey of lifelong learning.

As I end this time with you, I want you to remember these truths. I hope you carry them with you every moment of your life as you move forward. You are valuable, in fact the scripture says, you are MORE PRECIOUS THAN RUBIES!

The truth about me and you:

"I am created in God's image." (Gen. 1:27)
"I am fearfully and wonderfully made." (Ps. 139; 13, 14)
"I have a divine purpose." (Ps. 20: 4)
"I am loved by God." (John 3:16)
"God is for me not against me." (Rom. 8:31)
"I am surrounded with favor as a shield." (Ps. 5:12)

"I am more than a conqueror through Christ." (Rom. 8:37)
"God is my place of safety." (Ps. 91:2)
"Jesus is my friend." (John 15:15)
"Jesus is my peace and joy." (John 14:27. John 15:11)
"The Holy Spirit will guide me into all truth." (John 16:13)

I AM....loved, brave, free, beautiful, vibrant, worthy, healthy, bold, fun and enough!

You are my SUPERHERO! You are an OVERCOMER! You are MADE FOR MORE! Don't forget your place. Find your purpose, find your scripture, find your song! You are here for a reason, for such a time as this. God has a plan bigger than you can imagine! It's time to GO change the world with your BEST YES and the first part of that is taking care of YOU because YOU ARE MORE PRECIOUS THAN RUBIES!

XOXO,
Andrya Martin

The Whole Woman, Living a Transformed Life @ andryam.com

Andrya Martin is a wife, mom of five, grandmother of four and woman on a mission to help others fulfill their God-given destiny. She is the *CEO of Living Well, LLC.*, where she helps people reclaim their health with food, lifestyle and bio-frequency healing. She believes that you are fearfully and wonderfully made, called to a higher purpose and here to make a difference in this world. Andrya's expertise in Functional Nutrition, Cancer Prevention and Holistic Health Care Practices offers her clients a root cause resolution to many health challenges they are facing today.

Part 7: Methods that Monetize

I'll never forget when I got my first affiliate commission check. I realized that creating one post on social media brought money into my bank account that I didn't have to go "hustle" for. I was hooked.

What I love most about multiple streams of income is you do truly realize that the world is abundant and your ability to make money IS limitless. The fear goes away when you know you are in control of your finances. While it's not for the faint of heart and does take building in routines to ensure success, it can make a significant difference in your financial future.

If you're struggling to see yourself thriving in this environment, I want to challenge you to think of yourself as a multi-faceted entrepreneur with many passions. You may have come into the online space via network marketing but realize that you have fallen in love with coaching.

It's not either or…it's and. Don't forget that. Go about this with an open mind and you may be surprised at how many streams you can build up.

CHAPTER 28

List Leverage Lifestyle

by Lindsay Sewell

"Leverage is the reason some people become rich and others do not become rich."

- Robert Kiyosaki

There are people who will tell you that email marketing is dead. I may be a contrarian, but I believe if they think email is dead, it is only because they are not doing it correctly. I am here to show you that it is not only alive and well, but could become the single most leveraged and profitable aspect of your business when you take the steps I am about to share with you and apply it to your business and your list. Email marketing is the future, and the present - if you do it in the right ways.

If you are anything like me, you likely use social media to build your business. Social media has opened many doors for me; huge opportunities for exposure, the ability to reach a global audience and the power to search for and serve the people who are looking for solutions. I also realized early on that any platform I was utilizing for business that I did not have ownership over left me at the mercy of that platform (think: most social media apps). My business could be jeopardized or risk being closed down on a moment's notice with a hacked account, accidental violation of the platform's standards, or simply having a hater report my content. That is where the email list reigns supreme. You own it, you can take it with you, and you have full control over communication with your subscribers and community.

The power of email marketing dawned on me a few years ago when I decided to launch my first group coaching program. In full transparency, I was still a bit nervous to share this program with the world so I decided to solely launch it to my email list first before I ever posted about it on social media. In fact, I never ended up sharing it on social media. Because over the course of 48 hours, the entire program sold out. In total, I sent out four emails to my list. The small amount of time I dedicated towards this launch paid off through the power of my list.

Talk about life changing. This situation was when I realized that money can be created on demand when you have a list of people who know, like, and trust you. Building a rapport with your audience allows for familiarization and loyalty that has the potential to bring in sales. This allows you to stop leaning on only social media for your business. You simply have the ability to share your message and offers to hundreds, thousands - potentially even hundreds of thousands of people all at once without rejection. You're giving each individual the chance to select and learn more about the products, services and offers that your business can provide. All of this is the recipe for more time freedom and more financial freedom.

So, I know what you are thinking now. *How do I get started?* Let's dive into three simple but incredibly powerful strategies to bond your email list to you so they cannot help but open and read every one of your letters.

Step 1: **Make It Fun**

One of the biggest mistakes in business is trying to make the prospect understand the offer, instead of making the prospect feel understood. One of my favorite email marketers and copywriters, Ben Settle, coined the term "infotainment." It boils down to a combination of entertaining the reader and providing education at the same time. There is a reason that people do not sit down to read the dictionary cover to cover. It provides a great deal of information, but is completely lacking in the entertainment category. Your job as an email marketer is to make your letter informative and entertaining, while telling stories that allow your reader to feel understood, and at the same time provide them with solutions they need. Taking the time to make it fun will guarantee that not only do your emails get opened every time, but the readers stick around long enough to find something they want to buy from you.

Step 2: **Sell The Relationship, Not The Click**

Ever read an email that is just a direct pitch for the company or business? How did it make you feel? Did you feel valued? Did you trust the person or the business you received the letter from? Chances are it made you feel simply like a number. This goes hand-in-hand with step one where you share stories that entertain, inspire, and create a bond with your audience. You can sell in every letter, but every letter should also strengthen the relationship with your reader. If the focus is simply on selling the click each and every time, then before you know it, there will be no one left on the list to sell to. Teach your readers the things they desire to learn. Share stories that bond them to you and allow them to see themselves in the story. Offer contrarian views to open their minds and give them a new point of view. When you focus on building the relationship with your readers in every letter, then the sales come naturally when they see an offer they desire. And that brings us to our final step.

Step 3: **Consistency Beats Talent**

You may be reading this and thinking, but I am not a writer, how will I do this? I am here to tell you, I am not a writer either. I struggled through every paper I ever wrote in school. When I started my email list, I struggled through all of my initial letters. But this is the secret that no one else will tell you. Consistency beats talent. With consistency you will improve over time. With consistency you will build trust and your relationship with your list. Your readers will come to know you as a friend, rather than someone who only appears in their inbox once or twice a year during a big launch. With consistency you will get 1% better each and every day that you show up to write a letter to your readers. Your talent will improve over time, but your consistency muscle is what really matters.

Follow these three simple steps and you will look back a year from now and realize that you have the ability to make offers to hundreds, thousands or even hundreds of thousands of people all at once. Your business will change and grow if you follow this process. You can create the leverage, the time freedom and financial independence you dream of. I know, because I have done it, and I am passing this secret along to you next.

Lindsay Sewell is a business and marketing strategist and content creator who helps ambitious entrepreneurs to create a stand out personal brand online, build a profitable email list and turn a business idea or side gig into income faster.

After watching so many women and moms struggle in their own small businesses, she dedicates her time to teaching online business owners how to implement leveraged marketing systems to create more time freedom, consistent cash flow and make their online marketing fun again.

CHAPTER 29

Multiple Streams of Income

by Tori Edwards

Have you heard the buzz about multiple streams of income? Multiple streams of income refers to having income from more than one source rather than relying on a single source of income, such as a 9-5 salary paying job.

Having multiple streams of income can help provide a safety net in case one source of income dries up. This could be due to job loss, economic downturns, or unexpected expenses. It can also increase your earning potential and help you achieve financial goals faster. Additionally, it allows for more flexibility and freedom in your career choices. Not having financial stability can be scary but increasing your overall financial stability should include multiple streams of income without question. This will not only increase your income potential, but will provide greater flexibility and the ability to diversify investments and also reduce risk. Heck, it could also lead to a sense of fulfillment from pursuing multiple interests or passions.

Some more well-known examples of different types of income streams include salary or wages, rental income, interest income, dividend income, capital gains and business income. Identifying and pursuing additional income opportunities can involve researching potential side hustles or exploring new skills or services you can offer. Of course, you can build your income you currently bring in by asking for a raise or taking on extra hours at your current job, however diversification is key. Building income streams wide versus sinking all of your time and effort into just one will be the key to building faster.

Let's address some of the questions around how you can identify and pursue additional income opportunities, what challenges you may encounter, minimizing risks and maximizing potential earnings as well as what skills or resources are available to you. Of course, you will also want to research potential side hustles and explore any new skills or services that you could potentially offer. Networking and seeking out opportunities within your industry can also be helpful.

What types of challenges or drawbacks potentially arise when balancing multiple streams of income? Spreading yourself too thin and risking burnout, difficulty in managing and prioritizing tasks, potential conflicts of interest, and the need for strong time management and organizational skills are a few that are top of mind. Additionally, tax implications can become more complex when dealing with multiple income sources, but should not be the reason why you wouldn't take on additional income streams. You just need to plan, prepare and align yourself with a tax professional that specializes in the industries you are in or planning to be in. Forming a relationship with a good accounting team, bookkeeper, accountant, and CPA can actually save you money long term. Assembling a team around you, that will support your growing business with financial advice, tax planning and preparation, necessary audits and ensuring compliance as well as budgeting, forecasting and financial analysis to aid in any decision-making that needs to happen each month, quarter or year will be pivotal in assuring your business stays in a healthy state.

Another question comes up around how you can diversify your income streams to minimize risk and maximize potential earnings. You may consider investing in multiple sources of income such as rental properties, stocks, bonds, and side businesses. This helps to reduce your reliance on a single income source and can increase your earning potential. It is important to carefully evaluate the risks and potential returns of each investment before committing your resources.

The skills that might be required in developing additional income streams could include financial management, marketing, networking, time management and project management. Resources such as an online course, books, webinars, mentorship programs and business incubators can also be helpful. It is important to identify which skills and resources are most relevant to your specific income stream goals and invest in them accordingly.

There are unlimited options to taking on additional income streams, you just have to be open to really diving in. What I would recommend is to make a list, jot down everything you enjoy doing on a piece of paper, then jot down what brings you joy in life. Do this unfiltered, untimed, and uninterrupted if possible. Think about the different activities and experiences that interest you. Pay attention to how you feel during and after each of those activities that you write down. Keep writing until you have an extensive inclusive list.

Once you feel comfortable with your list, read it over and notice any patterns that jump out at you. Narrow down to about five or six ideas by making an outline considering if there is a demand for the product or service you are considering offering, how much time and effort you are willing to put into the side hustle, what are the potential earnings and does it align with your financial goals and can you market yourself and reach prospective clients effectively. Evaluating these factors will help you make an informed decision on which side hustle or income stream to pursue.

As you can see, having multiple streams of income is crucial in today's ever-changing economy. Relying on a single source of income can be risky and may be insufficient in meeting financial needs and goals. By diversifying income streams, you can navigate financial risks, increase your earning potential and create a more stable financial future. Multiple streams of income can also provide greater flexibility and freedom when evaluating career choices, work-life balance, and retirement planning. Ultimately, having multiple streams of income has the potential to lead to greater financial security and long-lasting financial success.

Tori Edwards is the Finance Manager at *Goal Digger Girl Co.* She is a mom of two and a wife to her amazing and supportive husband of 20 years! She has been an accountant for over 25 years, empowering business owners to gain clarity around their finances. Tori enjoys helping business owners eliminate the stress and dread of organizing business finances, providing them with detailed financial systems, incorporating automations with the focus on cash flow and forecasting - empowering them with the clarity and confidence they need to grow and scale their business. Outside of her passion for all things finances, she enjoys being outdoors running, hiking, biking and swimming and traveling with her family.

CHAPTER 30

Building Your Business from Your Backyard Up

by Gemma Sharp

You stand at the edge of the forest, pondering your options. To the right lies a familiar path, one you've walked countless times. It's well-trodden, clear, with visible twists and turns. The path is adorned with small stones and larger rocks, and the towering trees above allow streaks of sunlight to illuminate your way.

To your left, the forest appears dense and tightly packed. The trees seem to embrace each other, creating a path that is faint and overgrown. Thistles, bushes, and imposing boulders obstruct your view, casting dark and foreboding shadows.

As you contemplate both paths, a voice in your head speaks loudly, urging you to take the path on the right. It promises simplicity, familiarity, and safety, assuring you that countless others have taken this route before, making it predictable and secure.

But hush, listen... there's a soft whisper, a voice you've heard before but ignored. It rises when you quiet your mind, a nagging feeling from deep within your heart. You pause and start to listen, and your heart whispers back, *"Look at the path on the left. Yes, it may seem challenging and scary, but isn't that what you truly desire? Doesn't that thrilling fear actually make you feel alive? What if you followed your longing and took a step into the forest? You know it can be done. Others have taken this path, overcoming obstacles, carving their own way on their own terms. You can do this, just take that first step."*

"But what if?" you respond to the whisper. *"What if I can't do it? What if I get hurt by the thorns? What if I lack the strength to move those boulders? What if I get lost? What if I fail?"*

Your heart whispers back, *"But what if you succeed?"*

And so, at the edge of the forest, my journey began.

I wanted something more for myself and my family. I desired to create something unique, to have freedom in both time and finances, and to be the one in control of my own life. I believe you can relate to this feeling because you're reading this book.

As we embark on our journey as entrepreneurs, we encounter constant obstacles. If we have children, we must juggle multiple roles, adding another layer of complexity to the already challenging task of building a business.

Despite the struggles and challenges, building a business brings a special sense of excitement and fulfillment. The opportunity to create something meaningful, contribute to the family's financial stability, and serve as a positive role model for our children are all powerful motivators.

I started several businesses, including wedding and event planning and baby massage classes. When they didn't achieve the level of success I had hoped for, I became discouraged and gave up. However, by chance, a friend introduced me to network marketing. Initially, I resisted the idea of growing a business on social media due to a strong fear of rejection. But after some time, I began to question if I could make a viable business out of it. Despite feeling completely out of my comfort zone and plagued by "what if" questions, I took the first step.

I started following various leaders in the Network Marketing space and that's when I discovered Kimberly, *The Goal Digger Girl*. After following her for a year, I took the leap and enrolled in her *6 Figure Breakthrough* program. It was through this program that I learned how to grow my business authentically and organically online, and it felt amazing!

While immersed in the *6 Figure Breakthrough* course studies, Kimberly launched *Ignited Life Coaching* and that whispering voice of my heart spoke to me again. During a discovery call, Kimberly asked me about my passions, and I honestly shared that it wasn't network marketing that truly ignited my soul. It was actually helping struggling parents with their strong-willed, highly sensitive, anxious, and neurodivergent children – just like my own.

Kimberly encouraged me to take a bold step and create a business centered around my passion - a business built on support and service to parents facing similar struggles. However, this meant pivoting, changing my path, and focusing on something entirely different.

I found myself back at the edge of the forest, starting on a new path. Although I felt scared, I realized that I had accumulated numerous skills, and this time, I wasn't starting from scratch. It was like having a chainsaw instead of a hand saw to cut through the obstacles, even though there were still many big trees ahead. But with a burning passion in my belly and the ability to overcome obstacles with less resistance, I took that first step.

I continued to build my business in the online space, creating online programs and selling them worldwide. Then, one day, I realized that I had been neglecting a big market right in my own community - families on my own doorstep. I had been so focused on connecting with people through my phone that I had forgotten about the real people in my community who could benefit from my program as well.

I encourage you to take a moment and consider if there's an opportunity for you to work within your local community. Social media is undoubtedly powerful, but in-person human connection is priceless in today's world. Never underestimate the power of the local community and the opportunities it presents.

What I discovered was that when I connected with people in my local area, my following grew, recommendations flooded in, and opportunities multiplied. My *Mind Wizards* program has been implemented in local schools, I've been interviewed on local radio numerous times, and I was invited to become part of a focus group for companies on "Wellbeing in the Workplace," which ultimately led to being a guest speaker at a corporate event where over 80 local companies gathered at a conference. This was my first speaking engagement in front of 150 people.

The positive feedback I received was overwhelming, and it motivated me to create accredited courses on *Emotional Intelligence in the Workplace* for corporate companies. These courses are now offered in person or via webinars to companies worldwide.

The journey of entrepreneurship has been a roller coaster ride, and self-doubt and imposter syndrome have been constant companions. Thoughts like *"Who am I to think I can coach other parents when I find parenting such a struggle myself?"* and *"Who am I to think that I can break into the corporate space and coach CEOs of companies?"* have haunted me. If you allow doubt to take root, it will spread like a disease.

Imposter syndrome is a common struggle for many entrepreneurs, and mompreneurs are no exception. It's an internalized belief that one is not qualified or deserving of their success, leading to self-doubt and fear of being exposed as a fraud.

I've often let my lack of education, fear of rejection, and internal beliefs about my abilities hold me back. It has taken concentrated, consistent work to improve my mindset and change my internal beliefs.

Have you ever felt the sharp claws of imposter syndrome?

Overcoming imposter syndrome requires self-reflection, self-compassion, and a conscious effort to retrain the reticular activating system (RAS) - the part of the brain responsible for filtering information and focusing on what is important.

I find the brain fascinating, and understanding the RAS has helped me retrain my brain to see more opportunities in business. I want to share with you how to do the same.

Firstly, it's important to understand that the reticular activating system plays a crucial role in shaping our perceptions and beliefs. The RAS not only filters the vast amount of information our senses are exposed to every second but also prevents us from seeing anything that contradicts a core belief we have about ourselves. So, if you have a core belief that you are unlucky, your RAS will ensure you see all the examples of where you are unlucky, validating that belief. The opposite is also true. If you believe you are lucky, you will notice numerous examples of luck in your life.

This is how the RAS works. It helps you find what you're looking for, without discerning whether it's good or bad for you. So, when you're building your business, I encourage you to pause and examine your core beliefs about yourself.

Here are three steps to facilitate changing core beliefs:

Self-reflection and awareness: The first step in changing a core belief is to become aware of the belief itself and understand how it influences your thoughts, emotions, and behaviors. Take some time to reflect on the belief and examine its origins. Ask yourself questions like: Why do I hold this belief? What evidence supports or contradicts it? How does it impact my life and interactions with others? By gaining a deeper understanding of your core belief, you can start to identify its limitations or negative consequences.

Challenging and questioning the belief: Once you have identified the core belief and its impact on your life, it's important to challenge and question it. Seek evidence that contradicts or challenges the belief. Look for alternative perspectives, experiences, or information that provide a different viewpoint. Engage in critical thinking and ask yourself if the belief is based on facts or if it might be influenced by biases, limited information, or past experiences. Additionally, consider how the belief may be limiting your growth, especially in your business. By actively questioning and challenging the belief, you create space for new possibilities and alternative beliefs to emerge.

Replacing and reinforcing new beliefs: After challenging your core belief, it's time to introduce and reinforce new beliefs that align with your desired mindset and values. Identify positive and empowering beliefs that can replace the old one. These new beliefs should be supported by evidence, aligned with your values, and contribute to your personal growth and well-being. Affirmations, visualization, and positive self-talk can be helpful techniques to reinforce the new beliefs. Surround yourself with supportive and like-minded individuals who can help reinforce the new beliefs through encouragement and feedback. Over time, with consistent practice and reinforcement, the new beliefs can become ingrained in your mindset, replacing the old core belief.

Remember that changing core beliefs is a gradual process that requires patience, self-compassion, and persistence. However, I promise you that when you can master your mind, you can propel your business in directions you never thought were possible.

Don't be overwhelmed by the forest. With each step, you gather tools to help you cut down those trees and move the boulders. You're creating a path not only for yourself but also for others to follow, and you're changing lives with each step.

Remember, you are not alone in the forest; I'm in the thick of it with you cheering you on and together, with an amazing community of strong, determined and supportive women, you are changing the world!

Gemma Sharp is a professional with diverse roles, including being a wife, mother of two, emotional intelligence coach, speaker, and CEO of the *Hummingbird Life Academy*. Over the past four years, she has dedicated her time to researching and coaching parents, children, and teens on recognizing and effectively managing anxiety, emotions, and enhancing emotional intelligence within the family setting. Additionally, she extends her coaching expertise to the corporate environment, recognizing the profound impact that increased emotional intelligence can have on employees' mental health, productivity, and overall profits. Gemma is a CPD Accredited trainer, with accredited courses and her parenting course *'Mind Wizards* - Working Magic on Little Minds' is both CPD Accredited and Accredited by the ACOP *(Accreditation Council for Online Programs).*

CHAPTER 31

Flipping the Script

by Anja Grissom

It is way past time to flip the script on the traditional multilevel marketing schemes (MLMs). As a successful network marketer with over 15 years of experience, I help women live a life of purpose by staying motivated and working towards their greatest goals. As a former teacher, Licensed Professional Counselor, coach, and personal trainer, I know the value of hard work and dedication. Direct sales has allowed me to thrive in the business world, and I am excited to share my thoughts and story with you so it can open your eyes to new possibilities as well.

It is no secret that network marketing comes with its polarizing opinions. Before we dive into why this is the case, let's take a moment to define what network marketing, MLM, and direct sales actually are. I believe it's essential to clarify that these terms are not the same, and there are pros and cons to each. Understanding the differences can help us make more informed decisions when choosing a business opportunity.

In addition to discussing the different types of business models, I thought you would be interested in a brief history of MLMs and highlight current trends. I am excited to report that I have seen significant changes that have impacted how we do business in this industry. It's crucial to stay up to date on trends and be aware of the opportunities they present for growth and success.

Sharing our story is a vital part of marketing. You've heard it right? What's your WHY? *"Have a why that makes you cry."* Sound familiar? My personal journey as a single mom of three, who had to overcome adversity to achieve success is one of ups and downs, growth, blessings, and heartbreaks. I started in this industry in November 2008, very reluctantly, as a bit of a snob about the industry. I had three degrees and did not know a single person paying their bills from direct sales. Everyone I knew just sold their products to their family and friends at their discount. I ended up joining because I wanted "the deal." But then I fell in love with the products and became an advocate by sharing with my circle of people. Once the products cleared up my acne, I would get questions about my skincare process, and eventually, I also cleared up my debt. I have earned over 30 trips, several cars, and have helped 1000+ others to see the opportunity to make money. I don't say this to impress you but rather to show you all of the opportunities I've been given from being in the industry. Direct sales has been a significant factor in my personal and professional growth, and I want to pay it forward by sharing my story with others. I believe that anyone can achieve success with the right mindset, tools, and support.

Are you currently a part of an MLM or aspiring to be one? Either way it is important to understand the differences between MLM, network marketing, and affiliate marketing. MLMs rely on building a team of distributors to sell a product and make residual income off of their sales. Network marketing also relies on independent distributors to sell a product, but without the recruitment component. Affiliate marketing is where individuals promote and sell a company's product or service for a commission, without building a team of reps. Direct sales is an umbrella term to cover all of these and other terms being used such as 'social selling' which is a synonym for an MLM.

One issue that I have heard and can get companies in trouble, potentially even shut down, is false claims. Whether direct claims or implied claims, they are rampant in the industry and difficult to ignore. There are things we can learn from these claims, like how it is important to be transparent about the business model and ensure all participants fully understand the opportunity and potential challenges. By doing so, you can build trust and long-term relationships with your customers and distributors.

Burn out is a real thing in this industry. Leaders in the direct sales space are encouraged to work their personal business 80% of the time and work the "team business" for the remaining 20%. It can definitely be switched around – that is the beauty of this industry, you can make the business what you want. I've learned a lot since joining the online space years ago, and now I'm currently empowering, delegating, and automating rather than enabling. This has led to more success and not "grinding my face off" as my former mentor would constantly coach. I do not regret fully erring on the side of working hard to help others, however, if we want to live the dream we are selling, there is a better way to do so. I would advise you to provide proper training and support for new team members and set realistic expectations for their success. Additionally, understanding your target audience (AKA: avatar) and their demographic can help you tailor your marketing approach.

It is important to note that each company has its own onboarding process and level of support for new marketers, which can impact their success. Motivation, commitment, and consistency are key factors in determining how successful you can be. Success is not guaranteed. This is a mistake I've seen other network marketers make; success should not be implied that it is being promised. I found it very interesting in my research that MLMs have a diverse group of participants, including those with college degrees (66%) and no prior sales experience (60%); contrary to popular stereotypes. Over the years, I have seen people of all walks of life succeed and fail.

Pros of being in the industry:
• **Time Flexibility**: MLMs allow individuals to work from home and set their own schedule, which can be beneficial for those with other responsibilities and commitments.
• **Potential for high earnings**: While it is not a guarantee, there is potential to earn a significant income in an MLM if the individual puts in the effort and builds a strong network of customers and recruits.
• **Support**: Many MLM companies provide training and support to their independent distributors, which can be helpful for those new to the industry or entrepreneurship.

• **Investment**: Although it is still an investment, it is very low when compared to other business startups and is usually for the most part purchasing products for personal and/or business use. Most do not require or encourage inventory any longer. Some still have marketers send out samples, fliers, etc and may charge for a website and or apps. Overall, the overhead and investment to start is minimal.
• **Personal Development**: Most people come in and do more personal development than they were or would have by not being in the MLM industry.

Cons of the industry:
• **Pyramid scheme accusations**: MLMs are often accused of being pyramid schemes, which can taint the reputation of the company and its distributors.
• **Pressure to recruit**: While building a strong network is important for success in an MLM, there can be pressure to constantly recruit new members, which may not be sustainable or ethical in execution.
• **Limited control**: As an independent distributor, individuals have limited control over the products and marketing materials provided by the MLM company.
• **Potential for financial loss**: There is always a risk of financial loss in any business venture, including MLMs.

Individuals need to be cautious and do proper research before investing time and money into an MLM opportunity.

Red Flags to look out for:

- Too many products or not enough
- Products are not a monthly supply
- Not a residual income
- Carrying inventory
- Party plan
- The company doesn't allow multiple streams of income

What has changed recently:
• **Technology and Apps**: There are now many apps and websites which are providing an easier way to sell products. For example, apps like *Project Broadcast* for mass texting that is individualized and automated can set you apart from the competition.
• **Virtual Conferences and Training**: Many events have moved online which has given the industry a chance to be more inclusive, connect with a wider audience and learn

from experts all over the world. This has significantly increased reach.

• **Value-Based Marketing**: Direct sales business owners are getting social media training and learning they must stand out from the sea of options through providing value. Consumers want to know why they should give you their time and money. They want to be educated, entertained, and know exactly what's in it for them.

• **Mindful Marketing**: Customers are now more aware of how their purchases not only affect themselves, but also the environment. This has led to a rise in companies promoting eco-friendly and ethical products. Additionally, consumers are more aware of their own needs and look for products that match their health and wellness goals.

Overall, the industry is always evolving and it is important for business owners to stay up to date with current trends and practices. The key is to lead with integrity, provide value, and be genuine in all interactions with customers and team members.

Why do we still see the Spammy Tammy posts along with unethical practices in the MLM industry? This may be due to these individuals posting about what they "know" to be right, or are being taught incorrectly, or are simply unaware of best practices - and end up failing as a result. So, what can we do?

As a *Goal Digger* Business Concierge and a Certified Social Media Coach, I work with business owners every day to help them with their business plan and social media marketing. First off, it is important to complete your own research and due diligence before joining any MLM or affiliate program. Look for desirable attributes that are important to you and your family. I would suggest looking for a decent product offering, but not too large. In addition, I would seek out a company that is global, has consumable products, on trend with standards and marketing, and provides training and resources so you can actually work your business and not work 24/7. Secondly, if you are already part of an MLM or affiliate program, it's important to hold ourselves and our teams accountable to ethical practices. This includes not making false claims about products or income potential, being transparent about the business opportunity, and not pressuring people into joining, doing things our way, or staying if they're unhappy.

It's important to remember that our actions can greatly influence the perceptions and attitudes towards our industry as a whole. We should always strive to set high standards and be accountable for our actions. One way to do this is by following correct procedures and holding ourselves and others to the same standard. We should avoid setting unrealistic expectations for ourselves and others, and instead focus on providing genuine value when marketing. I have been a top seller and recruiter in three companies and I contribute that to hard work, consistency, and transparency. People can sense when you are honest and genuinely try to solve a problem for them; which is the definition of selling.

Think about your own experience and/or the experiences of others you know. Did anyone attempt to control what you did and didn't do with your business? I feel that it is imperative to remain respectful of others and understand that others are entitled to make their own decisions without being subjected to coercion. Companies should have clear policies and procedures that are enforced and provide training and resources to support their marketers. Unfortunately, this is not always the case. Unfortunately, there are unethical people in every arena, but this is NOT the vast majority of people in direct sales or in general.

Finally, I love buying from other small business owners and MLM business owners. How can we help as consumers? We should stay informed and be wary of marketing tactics that seem spammy or outdated. I love this industry and the thousands of people I have met because I am in direct sales. Even with the good, the bad, and the ugly I have experienced, I am incredibly grateful. I want to encourage all of us to do what we can to hold others accountable. If we come across inappropriate marketing practices, we should let the person know that their tactics are not welcomed or acceptable. When everyone is elevating our standards and being accountable for our actions, we can help change the negative attitudes towards the MLM industry and create a better, more ethical way of doing business; therefore, flipping the script for the better.

Anja Grissom is a seven-figure career earner helping other women build a life of freedom, impact, and financial independence as a Business Strategist for *Goal Digger Girl Co.* Anja is a teacher, therapist, and personal trainer turned Health and Wellness Social Marketer and Leader then, thanks to *Goal Digger Girl Co*, a Coach, Influencer, Podcaster, and Speaker. Anja has Teaching and Counseling Degrees (Masters plus) and LPC. She has 32 years of

Teaching/Coaching/Counseling/Mentoring Experience with 14 in NWM. Plus, Anja has completed the Social Media Coaching Certification with *Goal Digger*, been in the various coaching programs, and was the top *Goal Digger Influencer* for 2022 in only nine months. Anja is 52 and lives in Oklahoma as a divorced, single, empty nester mom of four: 19-year-old Kirby currently in college; 20-year-old Cayle working and living at home; plus a grown step daughter Ashley and grown adopted son Christian who is 22. It is Anja's passion to help other women, especially moms, become more confident and authentic versions of themselves, never settle for less than their best, and to achieve the highest level of success and wealth possible.

Part 8:

Essential

Business

Fundamentals

I agree this isn't the sexiest topic but I gotta tell you, when you learn how to become a true business woman, it really lights you up from the inside out.

For some reason there seems to be fear and resistance around the unknown when it comes to making sure our businesses are healthy, profitable and sustainable.

Wherever that comes from, I suggest we shift into a new paradigm of intimately knowing our numbers. In order to make decisions confidently and quickly, this is essential.

Now let's take a look at some nuts and bolts to building a successful, long-term business.

CHAPTER 32

Overcoming Limiting Beliefs to Build a Strong Business

by Lauren Buckner

Most business owners are unsuccessful and struggle because they lack three things: structure, systems, and belief. The latter of these three areas, lack of belief, is the most detrimental. Why? Belief is a fundamental pillar for business owners to achieve success. It serves as a driving force that fuels your passion, determination, and resilience. In essence, "belief" instills confidence, fosters innovation, and empowers you to navigate uncertainty while remaining committed to your purpose. This may shock you, but many business owners do not believe that they are worthy of success. Shocker, right?! It is true and quite unfortunate, because it is the kiss of death, your business cannot survive without your true belief that you can build a successful business.

The best way to dial into your belief is to practice **Personal Development;** this is the first tool needed to create a successful business. Personal development is the process of improving yourself, assessing your life goals and working on acquiring skills and values for your growth to maximize your potential. You must be consistent for this process to be effective; I encourage you to commit to at least 15-20 minutes of personal development each day (yes even Saturdays and Sundays). You can enhance your personal development skills in several ways, such as by reading or listening to self-empowerment books, subscribing to podcasts, working with a professional, journaling or meditating. The key is to commit to facing your fears and changing your mindset because the thing(s) that will hold you back in your business stems from one or more limiting beliefs; personal development will help you release those beliefs.

Listen, I know what I am talking about when it comes to the power of personal development…yes today I am a successful business and real estate attorney, business consultant and entrepreneur, but I was not always on a path that was destined to lead me here. I used to struggle with an extreme case of limiting beliefs. I really had to do a lot of work to open my mind to the possibility that I could be a business owner and not just a business owner, but a successful business owner of multiple businesses.

I come from a background of "lack." I grew up with an alcoholic mother with mental health issues and I struggled.

There's just no other way to say it. Poverty smacked me across the face. I experienced firsthand what it was like to live in homes with no water, no heat, no electricity. I know what it is like to have no food to eat except for the food that you can carry from the local food pantry and churches. I used to climb in and out of trash cans to collect cans for money to survive. Lack…poverty. People judged me negatively because of my circumstances and assumed the worst outcome for my life and projected those beliefs on me. My mother did everything she could to kill my spirit and to destroy who I was or who I would ever become. I just remember feeling so out of control and like nothing. That feeling stayed with me for what seemed like forever and although it initially fueled my desire to succeed, it was heavy and was not easy to shake. Between society's judgmental stories and the emotional and physical abuse from my mother, there was not a great expectation that I would amount to much…I sometimes even believed that.

And so, as I embarked on life and on my career and entrepreneurship journey, I struggled with my insecurities from the past. I struggled with feeling inadequate and not good enough. I struggled with the fear of not being successful. But through consistent personal development I was able to release those limiting beliefs and turn them into fuel to power my dynasty. Personal development freed me! The same will happen for you as you embark on your road of personal development. You will unleash so many things that have held you back and you will experience a sense of freedom which will make way for your sense of worthiness and will confirm that you most certainly deserve success.

After your mind is clear, you will be ready to start building your business blueprint, the next tool that I offer you is the **Business Plan.** You cannot skip this step. So many people downplay the importance of a business plan and skip this step…sadly enough I have watched their businesses crumble. That does not need to be you. Write this down on a sticky note: "*I am moving in the spirit of excellence; I will do everything necessary to build a strong business.*" Let this be one of your daily affirmations (part of personal development 😉).

As a business owner you cannot cut corners and expect your business to produce positive results. When you use a business plan correctly you will be able to clearly identify the following: 1) your business purpose; 2) your service and/or product; 3) your ideal client; and 4) the financial obligations and financial forecast for your business. The business plan is your business' foundation, everything else stems from the business plan. And just to take it full circle, it is much easier to foster a strong sense of "belief" when you can stand on a solid foundation. When I was young, I had a challenging time believing that things would get better because I couldn't find my footing in life, there was no stability. It is the same with business…when your business is shaky or built on quicksand it is much harder to tap into your belief tank. Build the foundation.

After the implementation of personal development and the creation of your business plan, the final tool I offer you is **Systems.** Having well-defined systems in place is crucial for your business' success as they provide structure, consistency, and efficiency, which in turn will enable you to execute tasks reliably and free up valuable time and energy for strategic decision-making. Translation: systems give you space to move in your genius and do your thing! Furthermore, systems allow you to scale and seamlessly delegate, ensuring that operations can be easily replicated and streamlined as your business grows. Every business, no matter the size, should have the following systems: 1) customer relationship management; 2) task/project management; 3) team information/customer communication; and 4) bookkeeping. With these systems in place, as well as a properly documented business plan, you will not have to put in 20-hour days, and you will have a solid business that is built to scale or sell.

Personal development, structure and systems are the tools I used to build multiple successful businesses. I now focus my time lifting up other female business owners and sharing my tools for success. I am known as the *Business Builder*, and I help women build strong businesses on solid foundations to leverage business income and create money babies!!! My dream for you and every other woman is that you have the skills and resources to tap into your next level and to create sustainable, income generating businesses. But the truth is that at the core of the success of your business is you; you must be committed and consistent in all that you do. You must understand that it is a journey and not a race, every step counts. Work on creating a daily personal development routine, take the time to work with a professional to outline your business plan and invest in systems. I know that you can do this, you have everything inside of you that you need. Ultimately it is the unwavering belief in yourself and in your ideas that will propel you forward and pave your way to success. Keep believing that everything is possible…you got this!

Lauren is an attorney-turned entrepreneur who works with women to help them build a financially, empowered life. Lauren is originally from St Louis, MO and attended *Cornell College* in Mt. Vernon, IA where she studied Psychology and Spanish. After college, Lauren moved to Bolivia, South America where she worked as an English professor and performed as a professional dancer with a Latin jazz company throughout the region. Lauren returned from Bolivia to attend law school at *St. Louis University School of Law* where she received her juris doctor in 2006 with an emphasis in International and Comparative Law. Lauren is a seasoned real estate development and business attorney and has specialized in affordable housing and mixed-use real estate developments transactions for the past 17 years. She is the owner of *Buckner Consulting*, a business consulting firm where she represents small and mid-sized companies in their general business matters, contract negotiation and land matters. Lauren is also the owner of *Body by Buckner*, a boutique wellness company where she helps busy, high achieving women learn to prioritize themselves and overcome emotional barriers to live healthy lives. Lauren has combined her in-depth knowledge of real estate development, finance and business to create her signature *Business Builder* community where she helps women build strong businesses on solid foundations to leverage income and create money babies!

Follow Lauren on social @laurenjalea on *Instagram* and *Facebook*: www.facebook.com/laurenbuckner22.

CHAPTER 33

Creating a Loyal Community

by Amy Oostveen

Creating a loyal community is one of the most impactful things that you can do in this world and it's one of the smartest business decisions you will ever make. And, yes, I said, *decisions.* We often think that a loyal community is created by its members, but we often forget that it's introduced, kept and maintained by its founder.

You can decide to create a loyal community by connection, being intentional, staying true to your "why," and loving what you've got with all your heart.

Gatherings, parties and events all include guests but they do not all necessarily contain community. We could step into a non-profit fundraiser, financially impact the organization, and never connect with a single soul. We could then go to a birthday celebration the next day, say hello, take a picture, but still never connect with anyone. Connection is key when we create a lasting and loyal community. Connection is the actual feeling that you belong, you matter, you are wanted. Your presence isn't just accounted for or noted, it's desired and cared for. Connection is when you leave the fundraiser with a strong emotion in your heart and your body. Connection is when you leave the birthday party with a memory behind the picture. Connection is when one of your clients from your brick-and-mortar business has to move over the weekend, asks for help, and has a handful of women from the studio show up at her house with no notice. It's when you hold a baby shower at your house and women from a retreat you went on show up for you to support you. Events like these happen because the women shared a connection with the woman moving, the woman hosting. They experience a journey together in a way where they healed through deep scars, talked about their fears, and broke through major barriers in some form or way - together, through connecting with one another.

You can decide to build this connection by being very intentional about the work you are doing inside of your community. Let's say I own a fitness studio. I hire five people to work for me and they each teach two classes one night per week. Our goal is to create three classes per night per instructor. I make sure everyone always knows that I am the owner, I am the best teacher, I've been here the longest, and I have the most knowledge, all of our marketing is about me and how great I am, etc. First of all, I shouldn't have hired five people - but that's another subject for another time. What I'm doing in this situation is showing my community that there isn't community. It's all about me. My intention is to build me, me, me, me. None of my students talk to each other or connect because they have a subconscious fear that someone else will take the spotlight away from "ME." My instructors don't feel strong or confident because I'm constantly overpowering them and being a 'know it all,' eventually, and probably very quickly, the business dies, the business fails, there is zero community left.

Now let's take a look at this from a different angle. Same scenario, but this time, you hire a trainer to come in to train your staff. You have everyone go through the training at the same time so connection can be made; you offer intentional goal-setting meetings where you set clear expectations and connect each person to others as needed for them to achieve their goals; you make sure that Mary who takes class on Monday has met Suzie who takes class on Thursday, because they are both married to firefighters and have two kids. You create the connection, you intentionally draw it together, and then you check in on it because you genuinely care how it's going. Just this year, we have two staff or former staff members getting married and either half or over half of their wedding party that is standing up for them, are from our community. Connect. Set your intention.

After you set your intention, it is imperative that you stay true to your "why." I drive this point home with all of my clients, in many episodes on my podcast, and even in my daily homeschool curriculum. I didn't have the most outlined business plan when I started my business and I didn't have it all together when I had each of my kids, but I sure did know the driving force behind why I was going to keep working at my business and keep growing as a mother. The first thing you need to do in any big situation in your life, especially business, is to ask yourself, *"Why?"* Don't ask yourself why you are doing this because your answer is going to be too generic. In fact, let's try something together. I want you to imagine your worst day. Go ahead and take at least five minutes and walk yourself through your worst morning ever. Come back when you get so scared that you can't think about it anymore.

Ok let's take the following scenario as an example: *You woke up late because your alarm didn't go off. Last night, you were so tired that you didn't wake up to pump in the middle of the night. Your child, who crawled in bed with you in the middle of the night without you realizing it, had an accident and the sheets are soaked. You roll to get out of bed smelling like soiled sheets, hoping to get in the shower before the baby wakes up and...nope! There's the cry. You aren't going to make it in and are cranky; you need to nurse anyway based on the night you had. You're quickly remembering that 9-5 job you let go of that allowed you to pay for a nanny and have some help. You're really starting to question why you started this business anyway.*

In this moment, in your worst morning moment, what is going to keep you going? Why are you going to muster up all of the energy you have and somehow even attempt to head into making breakfast? This situation is one of the times you must remember your why. Remembering your why is also going to be extremely necessary when you receive pushback, criticism, comparison, even opportunity. You must have your value and mission statement so tightened up that it aligns with your why and is THE driver in your business journey. It's going to be tough to stand your ground when someone wants you to change. You might feel alone when you stand up for your brand against harsh criticism.

What does this have to do with your loyal community? Everything. Staying true to your why sets you in motion to hold strong boundaries within your community limits. It shows your community that you are willing to stand up for yourself, for them, for all of you together. It creates respect between community members and allows them to see that the community matters. Respect builds love. Love offers connection. Connection reveals truth. Your truth is your why.

Your why is automatically connected to your heart and your heart is automatically connected to your business. People often tell us to separate business and personal and the truth is, I don't think that's possible and I don't think attempting that result drives a loyal community. People are loyal because they feel like they are seen, heard, wanted, desired, connected (as we talked about earlier) and THAT THEY MATTER. If you don't love what you're doing, stop doing it. Your people will feel your lack of patience because you won't have it. You won't be patient with the new person that is your first-time client. You will lack excitement in your client's journey because you are only focused on the numbers and results. You will be rid of understanding for your staff to navigate balance in their life. Emotions drive a loyal community. They can also ruin one faster than they built one so be careful how you use them! You have to love what you do so that you can feed into your why, being intentional and creating connection. Over the last few years in business, I have adjusted my approach to managing, owning, teaching, training. Of course, I talk about knowledge, of course certifications matter, but I've really pivoted to lead with emotions. Yes you got it right, lead with emotions. I know what you're thinking….

- well that sounds wimpy.
- I don't even understand that.
- I thought we were supposed to talk about what we knew as a business owner…

Truth is, I used to think those things too. But what I know to be true, is when I fell in love with my business all over again, I saw new things, I heard people's hearts. Now, I listen more and speak clearer. I give grace when it's needed and set boundaries when it's required. I lead with my heart in every interview I do and look for characteristics that I once passed over. This has led my staff and clients to do the same and has been the most beautiful journey I'm so grateful I get to witness. Love what you do and it's not like work. Love what you do and people will too.

Creating a loyal community takes connection, being intentional, staying true to your why, and loving what you've got with all your heart. It will take following these steps over and over again, not necessarily in this order, every time. Building this kind of community doesn't happen by accident. It's a decision you need to make and it's yours to make every single day. I said at the beginning of this chapter that creating a loyal community is one of the best business decisions you could ever make. Why? Because there is no stronger customer than the customer you already have and the customer that has a heart just like yours. Lead by example, watch the impact, and the money will come. I promise ;).

Amy Oostveen is the Founder and Owner of *Flirt Fitness GR & MK*, *Flirt Fitness Consulting* and *Flirt Fitness Franchising*. She is also a Business Strategist for female entrepreneurs where she holds her certification as a Business Strategist and holds over a decade of success, the creator of *Life Redesigned Podcast*, and a certified Social Media Expert. Amy builds a part time business with *Bravenly Global* and is the co-founder of *The Art of You Retreats*. She is a proud mother of two children, homeschool mama, Master Trainer for pole fitness certifications and loves the Lord with all of her heart.

CHAPTER 34

Money Management Tips

by Marissa Greco

I quit my corporate job eight years ago with no money in my bank account, to join my father's financial firm. I saw where my life was heading corporately, and I did not like it. I didn't want to experience financial struggle ever again in the future, so I decided to pursue a career in finance by studying and obtaining certifications to become a financial advisor. As someone who has helped many business owners with their finances over the last eight years and has personal investments totaling $1.3 million, I can say that starting a business from scratch is difficult, but managing finances as a business owner can be even more challenging. Without effective techniques and technologies, it can be hard to maintain financial stability.

The good news is that being a business owner can provide greater financial benefits compared to working a regular 9-5 job. The bad news is that your financial success is all up to you. That is why as your financial adviser for the next few minutes, my aim is to assist you in navigating the key elements of efficient money management that can lead your business to financial success. By adhering to a handful of straightforward money management tips, you can manage your finances effectively and position your business for prosperity. As someone who had zero dollars in her bank account not too long ago, I can tell you that cash flow is queen. As a business that provides services, I understood that taking my business online was necessary to increase my income and grow my business.

Kimberly Olson was the one who initially inspired me to grow my social media following, and we collaborated on developing a social media strategy. Although I'm not an expert, I've managed to gain 13,000 followers on *TikTok* in just a few months and have grown my *Facebook* group to 8,000 over a two-year period. Increasing visibility of my services has been crucial in elevating my income to levels exceeding six figures.

One of the essential tasks for a business owner is to develop a budget for your business. Having a budget will assist you in organizing your earnings and expenditures, making sure that you have enough funds to operate your business. Start by estimating your revenue and expenses for the year and be sure to include any recurring expenses like rent, utilities, and salaries. Once you have a budget in place, track your actual income and expenses each month, and adjust your budget as needed. One of my favorite budgeting methods is using a reverse budget. If you are unsure what a reverse budget is, it's quite straightforward. Instead of paying your expenses first, you make saving a priority and then spend the remaining funds accordingly. This means that you pay yourself first before allocating funds for your mortgage, utilities, and business expenses. You can set up an automatic payment into your savings or investments at the beginning of each month and achieve your goals right away. By implementing a reverse budget, you'll be setting yourself up for long-term success and stability in your business ventures. So why not give it a try? Your future self will thank you.

If you haven't already, open a separate bank account for your business to keep your personal and business finances separate. This will ensure that you are tracking all your business expenses and income separately from your personal transactions. It will also make it easier to prepare your tax returns and keep your business in compliance with tax laws. Cash flow refers to the amount of money that flows in and out of your business each month. Keeping track of your cash flow is essential to running a successful business. Ensure that you have enough cash reserves to cover unexpected expenses, and keep track of your accounts receivable so you can anticipate when funds will be coming in. A general guideline is to maintain a cash reserve equivalent to three to six months of your expenses. It is important to keep this money easily accessible. Consider opening a high-yield savings account to earn almost 20 times more than what you currently earn from your traditional bank and boost your cash. These banks operate online and offer higher interest rates due to their lower operating expenses. To ensure safety, choose an FDIC-insured bank and avoid depositing more than $250,000 if you have a single account.

As an entrepreneur, it can be tempting to hold on tight to your hard-earned profits. After all, who wouldn't want to see their bank account grow with each successful venture? However, investing your money is crucial in today's ever-changing business climate. By putting your funds to work, you can diversify your income streams, mitigate risk, and potentially see higher long-term returns on your investment. You want to create investments that can work harder for you and ultimately replace your income so that you no longer do not have to work if you do not want to! Starting to invest in a retirement account has the added benefit of putting money away for retirement while also reducing your taxes. There are many types of retirement accounts such as a SEP IRA, IRA, SIMPLE IRA, and 401(k) so you will want to make sure to talk to an expert before you choose the specific account.

Once you have transferred money into the account, now it's time to invest! Look to invest in diversified mutual funds for the long term. Investing in a mutual fund enables you to invest in multiple excellent companies at a reasonable price, with the guidance of a money manager who can handle the daily trading decisions on your behalf. With the right mindset and strategy, your investment can be the key to achieving sustainable growth and securing your financial future. So go ahead, take that leap of faith, and watch your money soar to new heights!

As a business owner, you put your heart and soul into building your company. However, have you ever considered what would happen if you suddenly became ill or injured, or worse yet, passed away unexpectedly? It's not something we like to think about, but having life, health, liability, and disability insurance is critical to protecting both yourself and your business. Life insurance can provide financial support for your loved ones if something happens to you, while health insurance ensures that you and your employees have access to medical care. Liability insurance protects you in case of lawsuits or accidents, and disability insurance can provide income if you are unable to work due to a disability. Protecting yourself and your business is not just a smart financial decision, but it also provides peace of mind so you can focus on growing your business with confidence. In today's business world, it's essential for women business owners to be financially savvy and literate. It's no secret that women often face unique challenges when it comes to money and investment decisions. Therefore, it's crucial to take a proactive approach and educate yourself about personal finance. As soon as I got educated, I was able to drastically increase my revenue and investments and you can too!

Understanding your finances will allow you to make informed decisions about your business's financial health and move forward with confidence. Don't be afraid to seek out resources, ask for advice, and network with other business owners who have similar goals. Empower yourself with financial knowledge, and you'll embark on a successful path towards financial success.

Marissa Greco is a licensed personal finance coach, educator, holistic retirement planner, and author of *Bottom Up Wealth*. She's been in the finance industry for six years where she currently helps over 300 clients and their families build long lasting wealth, as well as manage over $500 million in assets. A lack of financial resources and education for women led Marissa to the creation of *Invest Like A Woman*, where she helps equip prosperous female entrepreneurs with the knowledge and tools they need to achieve their financial dreams!

CHAPTER 35

Business Finances & Management

by Dr. Argie Nichols

We are living in a very different business world today than our parents or ancestors before them. Due to the events of 2020 and the pandemic, our so-called normal life disappeared completely. Our new normal became working from home to not working at all, as many were forced from their corporate jobs.

This process of being in-office to transitioning to WFH (work-from-home) life caused us to rethink our economy and our ways of life – specifically financial survival. During this time, we experienced an abundance of startups of small businesses. Unfortunately, many of these new businesses failed over the following three years. Yet, many survived and thrived. What might have made the difference? Understanding business finances and management made the difference. A strong, firm understanding of financial management is one of the main advantages of being a successful business owner.

Understanding the Benefits of Business Finances and Management

Quality financial management offers many benefits to a business owner. Sound financial business decisions form the foundation for reaching established business goals. Here are the important startup steps that you should follow when starting a new business. Let's get on the path to running successful businesses!

1. Write a business plan

A business plan is a working document. It is never final, and should be revisited annually, if not quarterly. This plan is a road map to success. It includes specifics about the company, goals, strategies, tactics, and more. A business plan outlines the specifics of potential obstacles and how to overcome those. Some can't be predicted, but the steps of how to handle obstacles, no matter what they are, should be established.

2. Form the company

You can create your company through the support of an attorney or CPAs. I highly suggest that you work with a professional to ensure there aren't any loopholes in your plan. Either type of professional will be able to guide you to the correct company type as well learning about taxation for your company structure.

3. Request an EIN and register the company

You will need to acquire an Employer Identification Number (EIN) and then register your company with your Secretary of State. This is an important step to keep you completely legal with the state and federal agencies.

4. Set up a bank account in your company name

You will need a business bank account. It is fine to use the same bank as your personal account, but you must keep the accounts separate. Before you can open a business account, you will need all the above listed paperwork from your company setup (name, type of corporation, EIN, address, etc.).

5. Apply for a business license from your city

If you live within city limits, you must check with the local government to see if a license is needed to operate. Most direct sales and/or coaching businesses usually don't need to follow this step. But it is always advisable to check with the local authorities.

6. Set up sales tax with the state – if applicable

Every state's requirement for sales tax is unique. You will need to check with your state agency to see if your business is required to collect sales tax from the buyer.

7. Locate your business office space – usually a dedicated room in your home

If you are a business that requires a physical location, then you need to complete research for finding the best space for you and your business. Your location may depend on the type of business you have; it needs to be within your budget, matching your brand, and allow you to connect to customers/vendors/suppliers. As a home-based business, check with your CPA for details and requirements for a dedicated office space.

8. Acquire insurance and bonding (depending on your profession)

You need to find an insurance broker (whom you trust),

determine your risks, determine any government/license/client insurance requirements, create a requirement sheet, fill out the forms and supplements, and give your broker time to quote it all. Approach it with goals in mind and an understanding of how it works. In certain professions, additional licenses may be needed.

9. Start using a bookkeeping software or hire someone
Bookkeeping is very important for your business. Consider getting special software or even hiring a bookkeeper that specializes in business applications.

10. Make sure your phones and internet are up to business speed
With today's technology, businesses can be easily operated if the internet and phone systems are up to speed. Find the technology that works best for your company, and make sure the providers fit within your business budget.

11. Create a personal brand – logo and colors
Marketing yourself and your business is very important. You

want to stand out and be professional. You may need to hire a graphic designer to work with you on this matter.

12. Have a professional headshot done and write or update your bio

The more you can do to promote yourself on a very professional level will just help make you and your company be successful. Once again, you need to make sure all these extra applications fit within your business budget.

13. Set POS (Point-of-Sale System)

A Point-of-Sale System is how you will collect money from the customer or client. Any website tools can be integrated to work for your business.

14. Create a website and setup social media plus other channels of promotion

Social Media Marketing is a very big business application in today's economy. There is a right way and a wrong way to do this successfully. If you feel weak in this area, you might consider specialized coaching on the topic.

15. Design and purchase professional business cards or social media ads

Business cards and digital business cards are important as they are easy ways to communicate your personal and business information to others. This will help you to build up the know like and trust factor with potential clients.

Financing Your Business

If your business growth requires financing (loans), then your management applications provide the needed information to know how much you can afford. You will have the needed documentation for the loan application and these papers will give you great strength to discuss your business circumstances with a loan officer. This will greatly improve your ability to secure a loan.

Budgeting

A budget is the first place to start your financial management practice. This is a tool to help you get and stay organized and to list all your monthly expenses and prediction of income. The main points of creating a budget include:
*Track all your business expenses
*Plan for the future

*Economize when you need to plan for expansion
*Make a profit

Introduction to Cash Flow and Cash Forecasting

Cash flow is defined as the balance of cash received less the amount of cash paid out over a period of time. Simply stated, it is moving cash in or out of a business.

Cash Flow Projection

A cash flow projection is a great business tool for setting sales goals and for planning for expenses. This tool is used to see if projected cash receipts will be sufficient to cover projected disbursements. This tool also helps to determine a breakeven point during a start-up or expansion. A cash flow projection is a very good way to prepare and plan for your financing needs and is often a required part of a business loan application.

Profit and Loss (P & L) Statement

A profit and loss (P&L) statement lets the owner of the business know if the business is profitable. The P&L is used to measure revenue and expenses over a month, quarter, or year. This statement also lets the owner know how well the business is being managed.

Summary

Being a business owner is a rewarding experience. Many people are leaving corporate America to "do their own thing." No matter what type of business you decide to start, the above listed points can be applied and will assist you in becoming a very profitable business person. The five key points to remember are:

1. Develop a professional business plan
2. Always start with a budget
3. Sound bookkeeping is required with the aid of a business CPA
4. Cash Flow Projections will help see cash shortages
5. Profit and Loss statement is the best tool for knowing if your business is profitable

You don't need a business degree to be a successful entrepreneur. You need to start with a dream, goals, and a strong business plan.

Dr. Argie Nell Nichols is a *Ramsey* Master Certified Financial Coach, social media Certified Specialist, High Performance Certified Leadership Coach, full professor with the *University of Arkansas* and a multi-six-Figure earner helping other women build a Legacy Through Financial Leadership.

A very family-oriented Christian individual, entrepreneur, lecturer, and author, Dr. Argie Nell Nichols's passion is helping students and women entrepreneurs unlock their personal goals. Her real-life experiences mixed with her love of teaching have generated hundreds of success stories.

She also speaks around the world inspiring leaders and entrepreneurs from many different areas.

CHAPTER 36

Your Relationship with Money

by Anna Pexa

Money mindset is a person's unique beliefs and attitudes about money. It drives your decisions about saving, spending, and handling money. As Idowu Koyenikan stated, *"The mind has a powerful way of attracting things that are in harmony with it, good and bad."* Research has shown that our mindset significantly impacts many areas of our lives, including academics, career success, and relationships. We will explore practical and powerful ways to shift your money mindset and open yourself up to new possibilities and financial abundance.

Your money mindset is pivotal in determining your financial success and overall well-being. It shapes your beliefs, attitudes, and behaviors around money, ultimately influencing your choices and actions. You can transform your money mindset from a lack mindset to a more positive and abundant money mindset. Having a lack money mindset is believing there is not enough money in the world. Abundant money mindset is about having a positive relationship with money, feeling empowered and open to the opportunities that your financial life presents. Let's explore how to fix your money mindset from lack to abundance.

Our experience around money forms our money mindset. I grew up with a single mom. Growing up, we didn't have a lot of money. I was working by the age of 13 to be able to get the clothes I wanted. I grew up with a lack money mindset. My mom did her best and showed us how to work hard to provide for those we love. However, the lack of money followed me into adulthood. I spent most of my 20s working two jobs and was still broke. As an adult, I had to file for bankruptcy twice. Yep, I said it twice. It's my dirty little secret. I am letting others know that if I can do this, you can too!

After the last time, I knew something needed to change. However, I needed to learn how to make the change. I did what I did best and worked. Yes, I could pay bills, but I still lived paycheck to paycheck. It wasn't until I learned about shifting my mindset that things started to shift. I was driving to work one day and listening to someone talk about making six figures. I said to myself, "*I could never make six figures.*" Then it dawned on me. I said to myself, "*I make six figures!!!*" That is when everything started to shift with my mindset around money.

Shifting from a lack mindset to a prosperity mindset takes effort, dedication, and a willingness to confront our limiting beliefs around money. I am someone who went from bankruptcy to earning six figures. I can attest that it's possible to rewrite your financial story by consciously shifting your money mindset. We all have the power to shape our journey, and it's up to us to decide how we want our story to unfold.

By changing your money mindset, you must develop an awareness of your current beliefs and attitudes toward money. Take some time for self-reflection and identify any negative or limiting beliefs you hold about money. Answer these questions that are related to money. What were your earliest experiences with money? I grew up with a single mom, and we didn't have a lot of money. I remember getting teased for wearing *Kmart* clothes. What did you hear about money from your family, friends, or society? If your parents said that money doesn't grow on trees, it could affect your money mindset. Even things like qualifying for free lunches can affect your money mindset. These things can affect how you view money and the amount of money you are worthy of. What beliefs do you currently hold about money and its availability? Do you believe you are not worthy of having an abundance of money? Are you living paycheck to paycheck? Do you feel you need more money to pay your bills? How do these beliefs affect your financial decisions and actions? By bringing these beliefs to light, you can consciously challenge and replace them with more empowering beliefs about money.

Reflect on the negative self-talk and limiting beliefs holding you back regarding money. Consider whether they're based on facts, assumptions, or negative feedback from others. Challenge these beliefs by seeking evidence that contradicts them. View things from a different perspective. Practicing positive talk around money is crucial to changing your money mindset.

Practicing gratitude is a powerful way to shift your money mindset. Cultivating gratitude for what you already have creates an abundance mindset. You will start to attract more positive experiences into your life. Take a few moments each day to express gratitude for the money you have, regardless of the amount. Focus on the abundance in your life, such as a roof over your head, food on the table, or a supportive relationship. Gratitude helps you shift your focus from scarcity to abundance. You are opening yourself up to more financial opportunities.

Cheer yourself on by focusing on your strengths and accomplishments, reminding yourself of your goals and aspirations. Use affirmations to reinforce positive thinking. Remember, changing your money mindset is a gradual process, but with persistence and dedication, you can achieve your goals and rewrite your story.

Identify and challenge any limiting beliefs you have about money. Common limiting beliefs include "*Money is evil,*" "*I'm not good with money,*" "*I am not worthy of a lot of money,*" or "*rich people are greedy.*" Once you recognize these beliefs, replace them with more empowering alternatives. For example, "*Money is a tool that allows me to make a positive impact in the world,*" "*I am capable of managing and growing my money wisely,*" or "*I am worthy of money.*" Repeat these affirmations regularly to rewire your subconscious mind and create new positive associations with money.

Surrounding yourself with people with a positive and abundant money mindset can significantly influence your beliefs and actions. Seek mentors, coaches, or friends who have achieved financial success and can provide guidance and support. Engage in communities or networks that promote wealth building and personal growth. Research has shown that the people we surround ourselves with significantly impact our success. Choose your friends wisely and start spending time with those who have the things you aspire to have in life. The power is yours to rewrite your story. You can do it by changing your mindset and surrounding yourself with positivity. By immersing yourself in an environment of abundance, you will naturally adopt a more empowering money mindset.

Every small step forward is one step closer to your goal. Imagine where you would be in twenty years if you keep moving forward. It's essential to set realistic goals and work towards achieving them. Breaking down big goals into smaller, achievable ones will help build confidence and motivate you. Remember, shifting your mindset takes time and practice. Make sure to take small steps and be consistent with your efforts. Embrace the power of positive thinking and watch as your mindset shifts and your life accelerates.

Changing your money mindset is a transformative journey that requires self-awareness, conscious effort, and consistent

practice. By becoming aware of your beliefs, practicing gratitude, embracing abundance, challenging limiting beliefs, and surrounding yourself with like-minded individuals, you can shift your relationship with money and unlock new levels of financial abundance. Remember, your mindset is the foundation for your financial success. With a positive and abundant money mindset, you can manifest a life of prosperity and fulfillment. *"The better you feel about money, the more money you magnetize to yourself."*
- Rhonda Byrne

Passionate about empowering ambitious women, Anna Pexa, RN MSN, guides them to excel in life and business. With firsthand experience as a wife, business owner, mother of three, and full-time registered nurse, she understands their unique challenges. Her expertise lies in fostering growth mindsets, improving organizational skills, and mastering time management strategies to help women kick ass in their businesses. Armed with a master's degree in nursing, specializing in leadership and management, Anna offers invaluable guidance to help women embrace their potential and achieve professional success. She is committed to uplifting and supporting women. She takes pride in propelling them to conquer challenges and achieve success.

Part 9: Trusting the Pivot

Well of course we need to talk about pivoting. I have yet to meet a client who came into our programs with one idea and stuck with it start to finish. Can you relate?

Feeling the need to pivot at some point is not only very common, it is necessary for growth. If we stay where we are doing the same thing we've always done, that isn't what we signed up for.

Because we are so creative, it is natural to want to explore different things. Just do some inner work to ask yourself if you are truly desiring to pivot or are just procrastinating on completing what you originally set out to do. There is a big difference between the two!

CHAPTER 37

Embracing the Pivot

by Lori Barthlow

In that sunlit room, surrounded by the serene beauty of the beach, I confronted the inner turmoil that had been plaguing me in my current business. I couldn't ignore the nagging feeling that something was amiss. Deep down, I knew that staying in this job wasn't aligned with my greater purpose and my desire to prioritize my family's well-being after a recent traumatic event we had experienced. The trust issues that had emerged as a result of one person's actions had cast a shadow over my perception of the entire industry and sport that I had grown up in. It felt like a betrayal of the utmost magnitude. How could I trust a sport, and an organization that had failed to protect what mattered most to me, my family?

As I returned to the beach house for the mastermind retreat, doubts gnawed at me, tempting me to retreat into silence, avoiding the vulnerability of sharing my truth. But I couldn't suppress my inner voice any longer. I had to speak up, to pour out my story and lay it bare before the circle of participants. I started by acknowledging my current business, but it was when I shifted the focus to my work as a coach in the athletic world that something ignited within me. Coaching and supporting athletes had always held a special place in my heart. Their mental game, their growth - it lit a fire within me that I couldn't ignore. In that pivotal moment, when someone astutely pointed out how my face illuminated and my passion overflowed whenever I spoke of coaching, it hit me like a thunderbolt. The realization reverberated through my being: my heart was no longer invested in my current business; it had become a mere survival mechanism.

Coaching, on the other hand, had been lingering in the background, patiently waiting for me to embrace it fully. A surge of empowerment, inspiration, and drive coursed through me as I acknowledged my true purpose. I recognized that I didn't have to be defined by my wounds or surrender my power to the person who had harmed my family. Instead of running away, I could embrace my passion, unleash my expertise, and make a positive impact on the lives of countless athletes. Although my healing journey was ongoing, the realization that I didn't need to abandon everything that brought me joy or shy away from my fears provided a newfound sense of vitality and purpose. I saw the opportunity to pivot, to redefine my path as a high-powered female entrepreneur who thrived on her own terms. No longer bound by the past, I vowed to live in the present, healing my wounds while harnessing my strength and allowing my brilliance to radiate brightly.

Within a week of making the decision to take this pivot, an exciting opportunity came my way. I was booked by a National Athletic Organization to speak with coaches about mental game readiness. It was a thrilling moment that propelled me into action. I quickly developed a business plan and created all the necessary programs, and the results were incredible. Unlike before, when I would often find myself stuck and frustrated, this time everything fell into place effortlessly. There was no steep learning curve holding me back. The feedback and momentum I received was truly amazing. Whenever I shared my work with friends, peers, and potential clients, the response was overwhelmingly positive. People who knew me well affirmed that this was the perfect fit for me, that it aligned with my natural abilities. It was an incredible confidence boost.

I felt a surge of excitement and a deep desire to give back to my community. The hesitation I had experienced with my previous business venture disappeared entirely. This pivot felt absolutely right. It was a wonderful feeling to approach every aspect of this new endeavor with enthusiasm and energy. Working on it was no longer a chore; it was uplifting and liberating. I welcomed the challenges that came my way, knowing that the time and effort I invested would be incredibly rewarding. Mental game coaching for high-performance athletes felt like an integral part of who I am. It wasn't just work; it was something I lived for, second only to my family. The inspiration to help athletes reach their full potential was overwhelming.

For the first time in a long while, my heart was filled with happiness for multiple reasons. First, I was able to manage my career in a way that allowed me to prioritize my family without missing a beat. Second, I was living my truth and doing the work that I believed I was meant to do on this earth. Even as I write these words, I am inspired to share my story and motivate others. The moral of my story serves as a profound reminder that even in the face of brokenness and pain, we have the remarkable ability to pivot and redirect our energies toward what truly fulfills us. It is within our power to forge a new path that not only enables us to be present for our families but also empowers us to make a significant impact in the lives of others. By embracing our passions, healing our wounds, and reclaiming our power, we can navigate the often challenging journey of entrepreneurship and radiate our brightest light.

Through our experiences, we learn that life may not always go as planned. We encounter setbacks, disappointments, and moments of doubt. However, it is in those moments of darkness that we discover our resilience and determination. We realize that our potential for growth and transformation is boundless. As we embark on the journey of self-discovery and pursue our true calling, we begin to understand that success is not solely measured by financial gains or societal expectations. Instead, it is about finding deep fulfillment and aligning our actions with our authentic selves. It is about making a positive difference in the lives of others, using our unique talents and abilities to uplift and inspire. Along this path, we encounter obstacles that test our resolve, but we do not falter. We recognize that setbacks are not signs of failure but rather opportunities for growth and learning. We embrace these challenges, knowing that they refine us and make us stronger.

Through our dedication and unwavering commitment, we emerge as entrepreneurs who are driven by passion and purpose. We radiate a contagious energy that ignites those around us, inspiring them to pursue their own dreams. By sharing our stories and experiences, we create a ripple effect of empowerment and transformation. In the end, it is through our resilience and ability to pivot that we uncover our true potential. We discover that even amidst the brokenness, we possess the strength to rise above and create a life that aligns with our deepest values. We learn that by embracing our passions, healing our wounds, and reclaiming our power, we can manifest a reality where both our personal fulfillment and our impact on others shine brightly.

Lori Barthlow is a distinguished CEO and Owner of *Mind Over Athlete, LLC*, an esteemed Mental Game Coaching practice tailored specifically for High Performance Athletes. With a wealth of experience spanning over 20 years, Lori brings an unrivaled expertise as a coach and mental game coach. Additionally, her extensive background in lifestyle-based health and wellness further enhances her ability to guide athletes towards holistic success. Lori embarked on her career as a certified sports massage therapist, establishing her own thriving private practice and traversing the United States to support athletes at various levels, including Olympic, para-Olympic, professional, and amateur. Having excelled as an All-American collegiate gymnast, Lori maintains a deep connection to the sport as the head coach for a local high school and *Junior Olympic Club* team. Education-wise, Lori holds a Bachelor's Degree in Health Science, a testament to her commitment to understanding the intricacies of human well-being. She further expanded her knowledge by earning a Master's Degree in Public Health with a concentration in Health Education and Health Behavior. Through her exceptional leadership, extensive athletic experience, and profound understanding of mental game coaching, Lori Barthlow empowers high-performance athletes to unlock their full potential and achieve remarkable success on and off the field.

CHAPTER 38

Pivoting Like a Boss

by Laura Caroffino

Alright fellow network marketing hustlers, just like one of our favorite Friends characters, sometimes you just need to yell "PIVOT." There are times when pivoting and creating space for change is necessary - i.e. when a compensation plan changes, you're feeling unhappy, when policy and procedure changes make you feel stuck. We are going to delve into how pivoting can be the answer and I'm going to share my personal story of shouting "PIVOT." When I saw others struggling and not winning, I knew it was time to start looking for other options. So, let's put on our sassy pants, draw inspiration from my personal journey, and discover how to pivot with style and determination.

The Wake-Up Call: Recognizing the Need to Pivot
Picture this: I was riding high, working my tail off, and reaping the rewards of my network marketing endeavors, walking the stage at conferences, earning all the trips, and having the top team sales volume. But then, boom…changes, and not such great ones! The company introduced a new compensation plan that left many of my

fellow consultants struggling to make ends meet. That was my wake-up call. Seeing others not winning made me realize that it was time to pivot and explore other opportunities. Sometimes company's make changes that aren't always for the benefit of the field, and as independent contractors that's when you have to decide if you can stay where you are or is it time to pivot? Change is scary especially when you're bringing in a significant monthly income.

And then the cracks in the foundation started to appear. Not only did the compensation plan change, but the policies and procedures changed and those changes weren't for the benefit of the consultant. The once supportive and empowering environment started to feel restrictive and suffocating. It felt as if we had golden handcuffs, if you will. When it becomes abundantly clear that staying put would only lead to frustration and limitations, it might be time to forge a new path, and PIVOT. With a shifting landscape, I knew it was time to find a new path that aligned with my values and ambitions.

Here are some strategies for a killer pivot. A key component in pivoting like a boss is to learn from the past, and doing what needs to be done to be confident in your decision. In the midst of uncertainty, I knew that market research would be my compass. I analyzed the trends, studied the competition, and examined the needs and desires of potential customers. I also took my time; I did NOT go to a new hyped up product launching company, it took me a long time to determine what company I was going to run with…two years to be exact. Armed with what knowledge I gained through research, I sought out alternative network marketing companies that not only offered a fair compensation plan but also had policies and procedures that supported growth and success. One thing that I've learned is sometimes we don't always get it right. Even if we do our due diligence and we choose a company that we truly believed to be the right one to partner with, it might end up not being all that we thought it would be. You don't know what you don't know until you're in it and running. It's ok to pivot again if necessary, but don't go chasing all the unicorns.

There comes a time when you have to embrace the power of change. When I found a new opportunity that aligned with my vision, it was time for a personal rebrand. I took a deep dive into understanding my unique strengths, values, and passions. With a fresh perspective, I revamped my personal brand and messaging, making sure it reflected my authenticity and magnetized the right audience. Rebranding empowered me to pivot with confidence and showcase my true boss babe essence.

Collaborations: Finding My Tribe

One thing I learned on my journey was the power of collaboration. Networking with like-minded individuals who shared my aspirations and values became my secret weapon. Together, we forged partnerships, shared insights, and lifted each other up. By aligning myself with a supportive and empowering community, I created a solid foundation for my pivot and set the stage for future success.

Embracing New Technologies: Innovating for Impact

In this digital era, technology reigns supreme. So, I embraced it with open arms. I leveraged automation tools, social media platforms, and cutting-edge communication systems to amplify my reach and streamline my business operations. By embracing new technologies, I harnessed their power to connect with a broader audience, engage with customers, and create a lasting impact in the network marketing world.

Facing Resistance: Defying the Naysayers

Pivoting isn't always a smooth ride. I faced resistance from those who believed I should stick it out and stay loyal to the old company. But, darling, I knew in my heart that my dreams deserved more. I silenced the naysayers, trusted my instincts, and followed the path that felt right for me. Overcoming resistance became a badge of honor as I stepped into my power and embraced the unknown. To overcome fear, it's time for a mindset shift. Embrace the idea that change brings growth and possibility. Recognize that the skills and knowledge you've acquired in your previous venture are transferable and valuable. Trust that you are capable of recreating success, and believe that this pivot is a stepping stone towards even greater achievements.

Embracing Growth: Lessons from Setbacks

Pivoting opened the door to growth and personal development. Along the way, I encountered setbacks and challenges, but each one became a valuable lesson. I embraced those moments of discomfort, learning from my mistakes, and refining my strategies. It was through these setbacks that I truly grew as a boss babe, honing my skills, and expanding my resilience.

Winning with a New Game Plan

The pivotal moment arrived when I saw my hard work pay off. With a fair compensation plan, supportive policies, and procedures, and a renewed sense of purpose, I began to thrive. My new network marketing venture allowed me to flourish, both personally and professionally. It was a true testament to the power of pivoting and refusing to settle for anything less than success. That's why we're in this industry because we are in this business to work for ourselves and when we aren't happy, we have the opportunity to pivot and win with a new game plan. I know that being focused, driven, and staying in my lane is what has helped me find success again.

Celebrating Victories: Owning the Network Marketing Stage

Darling, celebrating victories is a must! As you promote, own the network marketing stage, flaunt your achievements, and inspire others to take the leap of faith. There is a small caveat with celebrating victories, be sure you follow your policies and procedures when resigning from your previous company. If you have a non-compete you will want to make sure you're very careful on what you do on social media, but don't worry, you can still make a big splash without ruffling too many feathers! Through your success, you can be a beacon of hope and possibility for those seeking change. Celebrate every milestone, big or small, and let your triumphs fuel your passion for continuous growth and excellence.

Conclusion: Pivoting to Create Your Own Success Story

My journey in the network marketing industry taught me that pivoting is not just a necessity, but an opportunity for personal and professional transformation. When faced with changes in compensation plans and policies, I had a choice: to settle for mediocrity or to pivot and create my own success story. I chose the latter, and I hope that when faced with a similar choice, you choose to pivot too. I realized that after weighing all options, I couldn't continue where I was due to my personal ethics, and I needed to find another place where those I cared about could win again. Through market research, rebranding, collaborations, and embracing new technologies, I found my path to victory. Overcoming challenges and celebrating my wins, I emerged as a true boss babe, empowered to conquer the network marketing world on my own terms. So, my fellow hustlers, it's time to shout PIVOT! And be open to changing your path with style, sass, and determination. Embrace change, chase your dreams, and create your own success story in the network marketing industry. Whether you're pivoting from another company or your personal brand, you've got this, Boss Babe!

Since leaving her career as an Intelligence Analyst to become a stay-at-home mom, Laura Caroffino has been deeply involved in network marketing since 2007. As a proud military spouse and mother of five, she has found success as a top income earner for several companies. Laura's entrepreneurial mindset led her to build a nine-figure organization within three years with her previous company. Her unwavering passion for helping women build successful businesses has now led to her pivoting in a new direction, where she will focus on her coaching business. She aims to assist aspiring entrepreneurs in building a business that fits their lifestyle and goes wherever they go.

CHAPTER 39

Later is Greater

by Brenna Martin

Starting a new venture later in life can be a daunting prospect for anyone. For me, it was downright scary.

After spending 25 years in the corporate world, rising up the ranks to reach executive levels, I found myself at a crossroads. Did I want to continue climbing the corporate ladder, or did I want to pursue something entirely new and truly satisfied me?

At the age of 50, I made the bold decision to start my own business in online business management. It wasn't an easy decision, but I realized that if I didn't take the chance now, I might never have another opportunity to do so. Looking back, I can honestly say that it was the best decision I ever made.

Starting later in life has several advantages, especially for women. First and foremost, we have more experience and wisdom than younger individuals. We have learned how to navigate the business world, manage people, and solve complex problems. This knowledge is invaluable when starting a new venture, as it allows us to avoid common mistakes and make smarter decisions.

Another advantage of starting later in life is that we have a clearer understanding of what we want to achieve. We have had time to reflect on our goals and aspirations, and we know what we want out of life. This clarity of purpose can be a powerful motivator, helping us to stay focused and driven even in the face of challenges.

One of the advantages that I didn't anticipate was the support and encouragement that I received from other women entrepreneurs. I found that there is a strong community of women who are starting businesses later in life, and they are eager to help each other succeed. We share resources, offer advice, and celebrate each other's successes. It's a wonderful feeling to be part of this community, and I highly recommend seeking out similar networks for anyone who is considering starting a business.

Of course, starting a business at any age comes with its own set of challenges. For me, the biggest challenge was learning to be comfortable with taking risks. After spending so many years in the safety of the corporate world, it was a new and sometimes scary experience to strike out on my own. I recognized that I had to adapt to new technologies and trends, potentially face ageism and discrimination from younger colleagues and investors who assume that they are more capable or innovative. But I soon realized that taking risks is an essential part of entrepreneurship, and that sometimes you must be willing to take a chance on yourself in order to achieve your dreams.

To overcome these challenges, it's important for 'mature' entrepreneurs to stay up-to-date with new technologies and trends, and to embrace a mindset of lifelong learning. It's also important to seek out mentors and advisors who can provide guidance and support, and to build strong relationships with younger colleagues and investors who can bring fresh perspectives and ideas to the table.

Despite the challenges, starting my own business has been incredibly rewarding. I love being able to set my own schedule, make my own decisions, and see the direct impact of my work on my clients' businesses. It's a feeling of empowerment that I never experienced in the corporate world, and it's something that I will always be grateful for.

Brenna Martin, a seasoned corporate executive with over 25 years of invaluable experience, has harnessed her vast knowledge and expertise to embark on an extraordinary entrepreneurial journey. Her unwavering dedication, strategic mindset, and commitment served her well through the climb of the corporate ladder. Brenna soon discovered that her true passion lay in charting her own path and making a tangible impact beyond the confines of corporate structure. Inspiring readers to transcend their limiting beliefs, embrace their entrepreneurial spirit, and seize the opportunity to create a life of purpose, fulfillment, and extraordinary success. Embracing the philosophy that "later is greater."

CHAPTER 40

Creating a Life You Love

by Jennifer Mirt

Take a few moments to yourself and really think about where you are in life. Look into a mirror and ask yourself a few questions. Is your life fulfilling? Are you happy? Does your life give you flexibility to be with your family or enjoy activities? Do you have multiple streams of income in case something unfortunate happens? Are you able to save for the future? Can you honestly say that you love your life?

Happiness can take on so many forms, but you only have one life to live, so make the best of it! Your life will never change unless you do something different to change it. I often hear people say, "*I am too busy to do anything else*" or "*it is not the right time.*" Truth be told, you can always procrastinate or talk yourself out of anything. It will never be the perfect time, but if you genuinely want to change your life for the better, you just need to take a leap of faith.

Creating a life you love is all about discovering what you are passionate about, setting goals, and taking action to achieve those goals. I have included a few steps to help you get started on your journey.

A great place to start would be to create a vision board with all the things that bring you joy. Vision boards may be created in different ways, so do what works best for you. You could create a digital album on your cell phone or computer using tools or apps that you will see often, you could place pictures throughout your house on the fridge or bathroom mirror for example, or display a physical board that uses images and words cut out from magazines or other sources. Really think about what you would love to have in your life if nothing stood in the way: money, family, job, or education to name a few. You may include pictures of where you would love to live, images or quotes that represent your goals, pictures of a team you may have, images that inspire you and would be on your wish list for a genuinely happy life. You want goals and visions that motivate you, that maybe even scare you a little bit. You need to have an emotional connection. You want to create something that makes you want to jump out of bed every morning and get to work. So, think really big! This vision board will help to define your why and excite you to take control of your life. Having something to look at will inspire you and help you to stay focused on achieving your vision.

The next step would be to set clear goals. This will help to provide direction and focus. Make sure your goals are attainable, measurable, timely and align with your vision. When goal setting, you want to focus on what you want to achieve, rather than what you want to avoid. Stay positive, keep it personal, and prioritize your goals. Write down your goals so you can see them daily and develop a plan to achieve them. It will take time to reach your big goals, and as you grow, so will your vision. So be realistic and start with goals within your reach. Never be disappointed with small failures, you will have peaks and valleys along your journey. It is how you react to those failures that makes the difference. It is progress, not perfection. Rome wasn't built in a day, nor will you achieve your "big vision" in a day. Baby steps add up, so do something each and every day that will help you grow.

The next step would be to take action. As I mentioned before, there will never be a perfect time. You just need to start. You may learn by reading books, taking a course, finding a coach you trust, or listening to podcasts that focus on your goal. Networking with like-minded people who share your interests may also be helpful. You want to surround yourself with people who inspire you! The key is to just jump in and learn as you go. Do not waste time researching everything and procrastinating. True action is where you will find success. I love how Martin Luther King, Jr. said, "*You don't need to see the whole staircase, you just need to take the first step."* Always remember that we learn by doing, and the only way you fail is if you stop.

Along your journey towards your goals, you want to make sure you take care of yourself too. It helps to journal, meditate, eat healthy, and sleep well. You need to take care of your physical and mental well-being in order to focus on your goals. Physical activity is a terrific way to release endorphins (feel-good chemicals) that can improve your mental alertness, mood, and energy level. You also want to always try your best to remain positive. Find ways to turn failures into learning experiences. It often helps to take a walk with a friend and share ideas, or just to reinvigorate yourself. What you think about, you bring about! If you think you are going to fail, you probably will. So don't be a "Negative Nelly!"

When striving to reach that big vision, keep in mind that this is an ever-changing journey. You want to embrace change and learn from each and every experience. Do not be afraid to get out of your comfort zone. This is where you will always see the biggest changes. If you never ask, the answer will always be no! So, jump into the pool and have fun. Stay committed to your goals, be patient with yourself, and reward yourself along your journey to creating a life you love.

I want to share a little about my own personal journey. I have always been a hard-working, goal-oriented person. I have a successful career as a pharmacist, but I knew I wanted more for my life. I was tired of working for someone else and I wanted to do more on my terms. I was able to grow my health, beauty, and wellness business authentically, alongside my long hours as a pharmacist. I love to help people and I believe this has allowed me to communicate with others and gain their friendship and trust. After working hard for a few years, I was able to become a part time pharmacist. This has allowed me to have more time and financial freedom. I have been able to live a life of "get to" instead of a life of "have to," which makes me enjoy what I do so much more. I love being able to help others to make healthier choices and share opportunities that could help them even more. I continue to learn and grow my business every day. I am thankful for the knowledge I have gained through coaches and for giving me the tools to grow even more. Your dreams can become a reality if you focus on the goal.

Funny story, I honestly believe things happen for a reason. When I graduated from high school and was ready to head off to pharmacy school, my mother gave me a makeup mirror as a graduation gift. My sister had received a car as her graduation gift a few years earlier. (So not fair!) She said it was because my school was so much more expensive. In hindsight, I think she knew me very well. I was always into good skincare and cosmetics. Who would have thought my side business would have taken me into health, beauty, and wellness years later. I truly believe my mother is smiling down on me.

Follow your heart. You do not need to know how you will get to your end goal, but if your why is strong enough, you just have to trust that you will get there. So, grab that mirror, look into your eyes, and tell yourself, "*I believe in me!*" Never stop learning and growing. And yes, you can live a life you love!

Jennifer Mirt was born and raised just outside of Pittsburgh, PA. She obtained her pharmacist degree from *Duquesne University* and has always loved helping others. She enjoys spending time with her husband, highly active 11-year-old son, and furry child. Her passion is traveling and discovering new experiences. Jennifer knew she wanted more for her life, so she grew a health, beauty, and wellness business to give her more flexibility and choices. She writes about creating a life you love, filled with practical advice, goal setting, maintaining positivity, and overcoming obstacles. Jennifer truly is a life inspired pharmacist.

CHAPTER 41

Through Grief Came the Pivot

by Erin Roese

Grief is a funny thing. No one person deals with it the same, there is no timeline for when it's over and no instruction manual for how to handle it. I recently went through a miscarriage. The whole experience has been an eye and heart opening experience. I am now part of a club that I never wanted to be part of and I get it now. Why some people can't get out of bed, why it cripples them to their core and they are unable to function and how it can completely make life seem hopeless and dark. I cannot speak for anyone but myself and how I have been handling this grief…a loss of a child who I haven't held. A child who I never got to see their perfect little hands and feet. I want to share how I am able to get up every day and have joy in my heart and look for those beautiful moments in the pain.

How I am slowly walking through the feelings and pain.

The first week was definitely the hardest. The hormones were all over the place, my body didn't know what was going on and I had three sick kids while I was trying to hold it together. So what did I do? I cried. I cried every day at all times of the day. I remember going into the kitchen in between snacks and filling water cups and just standing, staring out the window with tears rolling down my face. Then wiping them away, taking a breath, saying a prayer for peace and going into the next room to deliver the goods to my three little blessings that always seemed to be needing me. That was the first step in walking through this: just letting those feelings come, sitting in them for a few minutes and then breathing with a prayer. Sometimes I have a hard time sitting in those emotions that come with things. I tend to push them down, suck it up and just move on. I couldn't do that this time. I had to deal with the emotions that would just come over me, randomly sometimes, it seemed with every little thing. A commercial or a post on *Facebook* about a baby being born. The sadness would come and I would let the tears come with it. Crying is a way you cleanse your soul.

Into the next week the tears still came and then the guilt. Guilt because at first I was not thrilled with being pregnant. When I found out, I was not over-the-moon, jump up and down happy. I have three kids; they are six, four and two. We are starting to come out of the season of diapers and nursing. I was excited, a little sad but looking forward to the next season of motherhood. So when I saw those two pink lines I felt worry, disappointment and disbelief. It took me a whole week to start to feel that excitement and joy. I had to accept that this was God's plan. He knew what he was doing and we were going to be fine. So once this happened the guilt crept in and stayed. It kept replaying over and over in my head: "*You got what you wanted, you get to have your body back for just you, you get to have a summer of no breastfeeding at the beach, you get to do all the things you wanted. You wanted this.*"

It was so hard at first to try to process and sort through these feelings. Normally I have to move and make my body work to help deal with emotions and I couldn't do that. The workouts I was doing stopped because my body was still healing and it didn't need to be pushed. So I started walking every day as much as I could by myself when my husband would arrive home after work. I remember walking with my snow gear on, hat pulled down so far over my face and coat pulled up to block the snowflakes that would pelt my face. The weather seemed to match how my soul was feeling every day. I would just let the tears flow, listen to my music and pray.

It took me over a month to work through the guilt and forgive myself for not feeling overjoyed at the first sight of the two pink lines. Every time the thought would come into my head

"*You wanted this,*" a little voice would whisper back: "*God had a plan, it is not your fault. You are loved, this is not your fault. I am holding you and want to take this heaviness from you, just give it to me and I will give you peace.*"

The verse that came into my head was John 14:27: "*Peace I leave with you; My peace I give to you. Not as the world gives do I give to you. Let not your heart be troubled, neither let them be afraid.*" And Mathew 11:28-30: "*Come to me, all you who are weary and burdened, and I will give you rest. Take my yoke upon you and learn from me, for I am gentle and humble in heart, and you will find rest for your souls. For my yoke is easy and my burden is light.*"

I wanted that rest so bad, the heaviness, the frustration, confusion, anger and sadness to just be lifted to be able to feel that peace.

I finally said those words out loud on one of those hard days on my walk. I just looked up with tears in my eyes and said: "*Just take this heaviness from me, I don't want to let this cloud my days and not let me see the good things, I don't want to carry this around anymore. I don't understand why this happened but please take this from me! I can't carry it alone anymore.*"

I felt a peace in my heart and the weight I had been carrying seemed just a little bit lighter. Praying and saying it out loud is so healing for your heart. There is something so powerful about saying words out loud; it is like an outlet for your soul. Giving your mind and body permission to let go of the things that you have been keeping locked up inside. Once I started to put these emotions and thoughts into words it changed how I could look at this chapter of my story.

Those were the first two things I had to do for myself to start walking through this grief. Move my body to get that happy juice going and let me work through those feelings even when I did not feel like going for a walk, I made myself. Then speaking those feelings out loud to release them from my mind and soul to let that healing begin. I don't think I am completely out of all of this yet. I'm still working on moving forward. Figuring out how to use this sad part of my story to help others, to make a difference in just one other woman's life who has been through this and struggling in motherhood. A verse that just kept flickering in and out of my head as I would walk and question; *"Why God? Why did this happen? I don't get it? Why would you give and then take away?"* Was Jeremiah 29:11 " *'For I know the plans I have for you,' declares the Lord, 'plans to prosper you and not to harm you, plans to give you hope and a future.'"* I have no idea what the bigger plan is but I started to feel that pull and tug in my heart to share this part of my motherhood journey with others. I prayed and prayed if this was the right thing and for strength to just be able to speak as I shared and not break down sobbing. As I prayed, it became more clear what I should do: start to share my story on social media.

The outpouring of messages and comments from other women was astounding! So many women saying this happened to me as well, thank you for sharing; I never have talked about it with anyone. They felt safe and seen to share with me. I kept praying and God kept bringing me these opportunities to share this chapter in my life with a story of hope and encouragement. I don't know exactly where it is going to go but I will keep sharing to encourage others who have been through this. That there is beauty in the pain. It doesn't seem like it now and it is so hard to find some days but there are bits of sunshine that flicker through. I am still walking in this, still processing, still letting things flow through. I am not sure when I will be able to speak about this and not cry or tear up and that's okay. There is no timeline. It is okay to not be okay some days. Some days it is easier to accept than others. Some days it's easier to think that maybe this is what led me to really share who I am and be able to connect with so many others who are hurting to offer hope. To let them know they are not alone. That is the hardest part is just sharing with someone else, being vulnerable to letting someone in to see what your heart is truly feeling. It is scary but also so very, very healing for my soul right now.

If you're reading this and you are walking in a storm of grief just know you are not alone. God is willing and ready to take this from you. You do not have to carry this oh so heavy burden alone. Just ask him to take it. He doesn't wave a magic wand and make it all go away but gives a peace in your heart to know you can make it through this life with joy after the storm is over. He will give you that strength to move forward on those hard days when it seems like the dark clouds are all around you. I also encourage you to share your soul and your story. Write it in a journal just for you, a letter to yourself, or speak it out loud or to someone you trust. Just seeing and saying the words will help you on those days to move through those feelings and release them. I am still moving and figuring it all out but I have hope and peace that this will not be just a sad part of my story. God will use it for something much greater than I could ever imagine. I cling to this hope every day and the peace in knowing that that little baby will never know pain, sadness or fear, but is safe in the arms of a loving God until I can be there to finally meet the perfect little angel that this baby is.

Thank you for allowing me to share this part of my story. Always remember you are loved, you have a purpose and there is a reason why you are here.

Erin Roese is a homeschooling mama of three littles; six, four and two, living in northern Vermont. She recently went through a miscarriage and has started on the journey back to the new version of herself. During this journey Erin has discovered a passion for helping mamas who have experienced a loss or hardship in motherhood, helping them on the journey back to the new version of themselves to regain their energy, joy and hope to see the rainbow at the end of the storm.

CHAPTER 42

The Importance of Lifelong Learning

by Leigh Ann Chiari

I had just returned home from graduating college, taking a few summer courses to prepare for the graduate program I had been accepted into, when I ran into an old boyfriend. We were catching up, telling each other our plans and next steps in life. When I mentioned that I would be going to Physical Therapy school in the fall, he said, *"Oh yeah, you've always really liked school."* I was very surprised and taken aback by that comment and responded, *"Well, if I want to be a physical therapist, that's the next step."* While yes, I had always done well in school, graduating right near the top of my class of over 350 students, I never thought of myself as "loving school." I was taught from a young age that to succeed in life, you need to get good grades and go to college. And while I know now that you don't necessarily have to go to college to be financially successful, (I know several men and women who didn't finish or even attend college making more money than those that did), I believe that you do need to keep learning throughout life. In order to be successful in life, you must continue to learn, add new skill sets to your toolbox, and continue to perfect the skills you already have.

Now let me tell you another story. I did attend and graduate from physical therapy school, got married, had 2.5 kids, bought a house…just living the American dream, right? What was so surprising though, was that after a few years, I was not finding joy in my day-to-day life. From the outside, I had gained everything I could ever want out of life. However, I felt stuck. While I loved helping my patients reach their functional physical goals, I was stagnant in my own personal growth. There was something inside of me, pulling at my heart, telling me that I needed something more. So, what options did I have? I could work on a specialty within my profession to become more of an expert in my field. I could enroll in the next level of education in my field, receive a doctorate and become a professor teaching physical therapy. I could even learn something totally different outside of my current profession, which to most, would seem like the least logical thing to do. Can you guess what I chose? While everyone around me was kindly suggesting that I stick with what I knew and pick a specialty within the physical therapy field, I chose option 3. I wanted to learn something new and different. I wanted to feel that excitement again that

I had as a physical therapy student, learning and experiencing something brand new.

Before I tell you what path I ended up going down, I want to point out something. Before I even made this choice of taking a new path, I felt the need for change and growth. If you're reading this book, I can bet you've felt that too, or you're feeling it right now, trying to figure out what the heck you're supposed to do next in life. Do you want to know how to figure it out? Well, let me tell you. The secret to finding out what you want out of life…to get unstuck from your current situation…is to be a lifelong student. Yep, you've got to keep learning, keep growing, and add to your knowledge base. Now before you start complaining about the thought of becoming a student again, you need to look at it from a new angle. No one is testing you. There are no specific deadlines you must meet. There is no one you need to turn in homework to. This is for YOU. All you need to do is be open to learning new things continually through life.

This can be sparked by events happening in your life right now. Maybe you've had a recent diagnosis and after researching and figuring out how to improve your health, you find that you now have a passion for teaching and helping others do the same. Maybe you decide to have a date night with your spouse and do a cooking class together and you realize that you actually love cooking and want to host dinner parties regularly, write a cookbook, or even open a restaurant. Maybe you had an intern come into your office and after mentoring them, realized you love teaching those coming into your field. Or maybe you have witnessed an injustice to yourself or others and decide you want to be an advocate for that specific group of people. Do you see how being open to new learning opportunities can propel you down a new path that you never knew that you would love and have a passion for? Having continual new learning experiences in life can help you find that joy you've been searching for. This is why being a lifelong learner is so imperative. If you stay stuck doing the same thing, day in and day out, for the rest of your life, you are missing out on not only finding that joy and living a more fulfilled life, but also potentially making an impact on others.

So, what did I end up doing? Well, because I was open to learning new things, this physical therapist branched off into the field of coaching and social media marketing! Who would have thought?! Not me. I'm still so surprised how far I've come. What's so interesting is that by being open to learning one new thing, in my case it was network marketing, it brought me to investing in a social media coach to learn best practices, which then led to the opportunity of being a *Goal Digger* Coach within that same coaching program, and now selling my own courses and being sought out to help others with their social media marketing. I never dreamed that this was the path that I would go down, but I have found that joy and spark again that I had back as a physical therapy student. Lifelong learning has literally changed my life. And it can impact yours as well. I want to leave you with this quote that is attributed to Michelangelo, the great Renaissance artist, that he supposedly stated at the age of 87, "*I am still learning.*" You are never too old to learn. I believe lifelong learning allows for a more fulfilled life as well as the opportunity to make an impact on others. So, what is your next move? What new learning experience are you going to seek out? Never stop learning. Never stop growing.

Leigh Ann Chiari coaches health and fitness entrepreneurs how to monetize their online business with social media strategies to stand out above the noise! She has built multiple streams of income all while being a busy Mom of two and a physical therapist. Leigh Ann is the creator of the *Fit in 15 Studio, Fit Possible* audio course, and *Health Coach Studio* podcast as well as a health and wellness social brand marketer and Certified Master Coach with *Goal Digger Girl Co.* She encourages you to take imperfect action so you can impact lives!

Part 10: Unleashing Your Potential

My hope at this point in the book is you are starting to see that we collectively get to redefine success. It isn't about making more money than the woman next to you or having your social channels look better than everyone else.

It's about unleashing YOUR potential. What does the best version of yourself look like? How can you really show up in this world…fully and completely?

I know for me, a truly pivotal moment as an entrepreneur came when I realized I was never going to "arrive." There was never going to be this moment when I crossed the finish line and I could check off the last box on my to-do list and be done.

Life is all about continuing to learn, grow, explore and then pass that on in the way that makes us feel alive. Let's close out this book taking a closer look at what unleashing your potential can look like.

CHAPTER 43

She Believed She Could

by Tracy Lane

Old school network marketing gave me PTSD.

You know the kind where you have to call all of your friends and family up and invite them to host parties? Yeah, that kind. I'm not really a social person - at least not in person. I get easily worn out and hosting parties and begging people to come by was exhausting and unfulfilling. At this point you might be wondering how I ended up in this book. Let's talk about how I went from PTSD and swearing off network marketing to becoming a top seller and social media influencer.

I'm not new to running my own business - I started out in real estate and ran a brick-and-mortar business with my husband. I loved helping people and making sales but everything shifted after we got pregnant after four years of trying. I found my heart aching having to spend nights and weekends away from my family and I knew I needed to change something.

It was around that time that I was approached by a friend who worked with an MLM. It had been years since I'd looked at this type of business model for anything other than kitnapping- I just wanted a deal on products with no intention of selling. So when I asked about that as an option she said the company didn't offer a discount to consultants. You know what my first thought was? *"Then why would anybody sell it?"*

I laugh even thinking about it; I was so caught up on my previous experiences I almost missed it. Once she convinced me to look at the comp plan and shared with me how everything had shifted away from home parties and into this incredible online model, I really started to get excited. I remember feeling myself slip out of fear and into possibility thinking, *"Oh my goodness, if I could make decent money sitting at home nursing my baby, how amazing would that be?"* After hemming and hawing for a day or two, I looked at that $500 startup cost and said, *"What do I have to lose?"*

I signed up and was as coachable as could be. I listened to top earners and did what they said. I ended up loving it and found I just had a knack for connecting with people online- I liked showing up online and authentically sharing my life.

I'm not someone who does things half way - I'm constantly jumping all in. I like to challenge myself. When it came to social media and figuring out how to grow this business, I would look at the trends, see what's popping off, and go for it. When short-form video came out it was a whole new ball game, so different from the live videos I was used to doing. There was definitely a learning curve but instead of shying away from that I forced myself to learn it by committing to one reel a day for 90 days. I didn't care if I had huge results or no results, I was committed.

I always have these words in the back of my mind whenever I venture into a new type of content: *embrace the suck.*

My first reel sucked and it was okay. *It wasn't about being perfect, it was about making progress.* The way I looked at it as if there was no losing because I was going to learn either way, whether the reel was successful or it flopped. Guess what? Even with being consistent I didn't see results after the 90 days of posting. I still had less than 500 followers on *Instagram*.

I was seeing some growth on *TikTok* and *Facebook* but was truly shadow banned on *Instagram* due to sharing some of my beliefs. So when people searched my name they couldn't find me, they wouldn't let me be tagged in stories and if someone wanted to share something of mine a little notice would pop up saying something about how my content couldn't be shared because I spread "disinformation". Because of all that I made sure I wasn't putting all my eggs in the *Instagram* basket. I'm a big believer in repurposing content: if I'm going to create a reel, I'm going to post it in all the places. *TikTok, Instagram, Facebook.* It takes an extra five minutes to repurpose content so I did!

So there I was just doing my best to be consistent, to do the thing, and I start making headway in this new business. At first, $500 a month was amazing, then it was a thousand dollars a month and then I got to the point where I wanted more. It wasn't enough just to be able to do a fun trip, I wanted to be able to help the people around me who were hurting, move into a bigger house, pay down debt and give my kids more opportunities. So I knew I wanted more but my business was stalling. That's scary, right? When you feel like you're stuck and you can't move past a certain point that you've hit, almost like there's this glass ceiling above you that you can't see but it's solid. That's when I realized it was time to get some coaching. It started with a coach that cost a thousand dollars for three months and I worked my way up as my business grew and eventually had the honor and privilege of hiring Kimberly who is, in my opinion, the best of the best.

I'm a huge fan of finding a coach you trust, especially if you're starting to feel that glass ceiling effect, it's time. The biggest thing I got from coaching was that my coaches saw gifts and potential in me that I couldn't. They recognized my greatness. It was hard for me but I started to ask myself, "*If they see that, it must be there. What if I act on it even though I don't see it yet?*" I had to actively work towards believing I had it in me but I used their belief in me as a stepping stone.

The biggest thing was recognizing I didn't have to be anybody other than myself. When I started stepping into my own authenticity, that is when my brand really exploded. I quit thinking, "*I need to try and be like her*" and "*I need to do what she's doing*" and instead started showing up as *me*. I'm a little bit quirky, I'm really forgetful, and I'm always running late. There's so much to who I am, and I just started sharing that and I found out that there are a lot of women like me out there and those are the people that I connect with and *they trust me*. That's really what sales is. It's just showing people you so they get to know, like, and trust you.

And you can't do that unless you're being yourself.

So I quit trying to be everything for everyone. I chose to be myself, even sharing my politics and my beliefs. I had leaders say to me, *"Don't do that. Stay away from it."* You hear that a lot in this industry - don't make waves, just show up and share your product and keep your mouth shut about anything controversial. But I didn't want to connect with people if I had to hide the things that mattered to me. My faith in Jesus Christ and my conservative beliefs are a huge part of who I am. I found myself praying and asking, *"Lord, what am I supposed to do here? I want to be successful but I want to be authentic in honoring you too. How can I do both?"*

God answered that prayer by allowing me to stumble across a podcast series called *"God wants you to succeed,"* by Andrew Womack. It was a week's worth of teachings on leaning into your giftings and your abilities and the things that He has laid on your heart. Those things you can sense in your spirit. I started to realize God gave me my passions to share. I realized it was okay to show up authentically as me and wanted to show up online the same way I did with my family and friends. Despite the leaders advising me against it I knew I was supposed to be sharing all the things that made me who I am. I needed to stand up for my God and my beliefs.

Once I realized that building my business wasn't about what the masses think of me but about how I was honoring what God called me to do and standing up for the truths that He had instilled in me, everything shifted and actually became easier. That doesn't mean it wasn't scary. It was, and it took faith to not worry about impressing people or trying to be vanilla. The Bible talks about how we're not supposed to be lukewarm. I had to make the decision that no matter what it cost me as far as followers or finances, I was going to do what I felt God was calling me to do. I committed and as He is always, He was faithful and my business exploded.

Apparently when you have God on your side and you're consistent as heck, you can even beat the *Instagram* algorithm! I went from under a thousand followers to over a hundred thousand followers in less than a year. I've been able to find the people who really agree and appreciate that I'm open and share my heart. It's created an incredible relationship between myself and my followers that carries over into them trusting me with the products that I recommend.

I still do a reel daily unless there's some extreme circumstance where I can't, when I don't have it in me to create something, and on those days I have something else to put out because I batch content on up days, and then I just continue showing up authentically in my stories.

I've learned not to get too wrapped up in stats. If my story or reel views or even my sales are down, I refuse to let that get in my head. I've been doing this long enough to know that it ebbs and flows. I know that if I'm down this month, I'll probably be up next month. That has come with coaching and all the mindset work. You can't let one week or one month define you, you just have to keep on staying persistent. Consistency is key, always.

Here's the deal: *never* count yourself out, you go on and keep sharing your content, because you never know where things are going to take off. One of my first mentors said, "*Who cares if it takes you one year, five years, 10 years, that time is gonna pass anyway.*" If you truly believe that this is what you're called to do, then there are people out there that need to connect with *you*.

There are people out there that God has for you to reach and if you don't show up and share your truth, your product, your solution to their problem, nobody's going to reach them because God intended for you to reach them. Trust me on this: it doesn't matter how many followers I have, there are people that can watch every single one of my reels and they're never going to connect with me, but they see one of yours and they see themselves in you, they're going to buy from you instead of me.

I have been so incredibly grateful for this business and this online community. Because of all of this I was able to retire from real estate and sell our brick-and-mortar business. I get to be home full-time doing what I love. I can give to those in need. My kids have opportunities they never would have and I even got the bigger house. Next month we are closing on our acreage and I have a designer and contractor lined up to turn the home on that property into my dream house. This life would not have been possible without network marketing and the amazing opportunity social media has provided but even more than that, it's been because of my willingness to honor God and the blessing he's bestowed on my business because of that. I truly hope you found some hope and encouragement in reading this and that you feel empowered to be everything God made you to be!

Tracy Lane is an award-winning Network Marketing Top Seller and Beauty Influencer with over 300K followers across social media. She is passionate about helping others find their beauty and feeling seen and loved, while always prioritizing her roles as a mom, wife and Jesus follower.

CHAPTER 44

Setting Your Soul on Fire

by Dr. Kimberly Olson

"Be fearless in the pursuit of what sets your soul on fire."
- Jennifer Lee

In closing, I want to encourage you to keep working on your life and pursuing your dreams, until you are living the life you've always envisioned.

Most entrepreneurs go through the motions, just trying to make it through the day. Then one day they wake up and realize nothing changed. They and their circumstances are exactly the same.

But not you.

You want more. And I know this because you picked up this book for a reason.

And I know in my heart that you *deserve* to have everything you want in your life and more.

You can make a difference in this world by building an incredible business full of passion and purpose. You can make a difference in this world by shining your light bright. You can make a difference by showing up as your best self.

You can inspire others.

You can empower others.

You can truly make a difference.

There will be setbacks and challenges, but as long as you have set clear goals that light you up, you'll come out on top.

You are resilient.

You are persistent.

And you have grit.

That is the magic formula, my friend.

I used to live in fear. I used to doubt myself so much, I wouldn't even try anything new. I wouldn't take risks. I felt like an imposter.

And every morning I woke up with regret, knowing already before the day had even begun, that I wasn't going to pursue my dreams. I felt dead inside. My soul was barely a whisper.

But I got help. I worked on my mindset *every* single day and began taking imperfect action. I decided I was never going to feel ready and gave myself permission to fail.

And that decision literally changed the trajectory of my life. I hope that you go back and read your favorite parts of this collection again so that you are reminded you can do this. You are not alone. You have a tribe of *#ElephantSisters* and we have your back, during all the ups and downs of entrepreneurship.

No matter what happens or what thoughts come your way that don't support you, remember this:

"It is not the critic who counts; not the man who points out how the strong man stumbles, or where the doer of deeds could have done them better. The credit belongs to the man who is actually in the arena, whose face is marred by dust and sweat and blood; who strives valiantly; who errs, who comes short again and again, because there is no effort without error and shortcoming; but who does actually strive to do the deeds; who knows great enthusiasms, the great devotions; who spends himself in a worthy cause; who at the best knows in the end the triumph of high achievement, and who at the worst, if he fails, at least fails while daring

greatly, so that his place shall never be with those cold and timid souls who neither know victory nor defeat."

– Theodore Roosevelt, the Man in the Arena. Delivered at the Sorbonne (Paris) on April 23rd, 1910.

Cheers, My Friend

It was an absolute honor to put this book collaboration together. I know some of the suggestions included may make you feel very vulnerable and ask you to take some scary steps. I know this is just the beginning and my hope for you is that you continue to work on yourself because I believe in you, I think you're awesome and I know that you are absolutely worth it. We may not know each other personally, but we have been energetically attracted to one another, and because of that, I know your heart.

I've said this before and I'll say it again: it's time to stand up for your dreams. It's time to stand up for your happiness. It's time to fight for your life, look in the mirror and say, "*I want more. I demand more. I am creating more today.*"

I know you will do this and more because YOU are a Goal Digger.

Goal Digger *[Noun]: A driven person who's ready to #getLIT in her business, ignite her life and set her soul on fire! - Dr. Kimberly Olson*

ABOUT THE AUTHOR

Dr. Kimberly Olson is a self-made multimillionaire and the creator of *Goal Digger Girl Co*, where she serves female entrepreneurs by teaching them simple systems and online strategies in sales and marketing.

Most recently, she received the honor of being chosen as the '*Top Business Innovative of the Year*' by the International Association of Top Professionals. Kimberly has been featured on the cover of Success Pitchers Magazine as a '*Self Made Social Media Mogul*,' as well as '*Top 10 Most Ambitious Women in Business to Follow.*' She is a TEDx speaker and her recent speech was listed as one of the '*10 Top TEDx Talks that You Don't Want to Miss.*'

Kimberly is also the founder of the non-profit, *Elephant Sisters* and has two PhDs in Natural Health and Holistic Nutrition. She is the author of seven books including several #1 international best-sellers, has a top 25 rated podcast in marketing with over 700,000 downloads and has reached the top half percent globally in network marketing. Most recently she has shared the stage with **Rachel Hollis, Erin King, Keri Ford** and **Jessica Higdon.**

She is a busy mom of two and lives in Austin, Texas with her husband, Scott. Her favorite thing about being a mompreneur is being able to take care of her family while building an empire. And of course, she also loves teaching others how to follow their dreams, crush their goals and create the life they've always wanted.

Stay Connected

Her Courses: https://TheGoalDiggerGirl.com/services

Facebook™ *@TheGoalDiggerGirl*

Instagram™ *@TheGoalDiggerGirl*

TikTok™ *@TheGoalDiggerGirl*

YouTube™ *@TheGoalDiggerGirl*

LinkedIn™ *@TheGoalDiggerGirl*

Twitter™ *@Goal_DiggerGirl*

Pinterest™ *@GoalDiggerGirl*

TheGoalDiggerGirl.com